The Focal Guide to
PHOTOGRAPHY AND THE LAW

The Focal Guide to
PHOTOGRAPHY AND THE LAW

Adrian Berkeley LLB FRSA

Focal Press
An imprint of Butterworth-Heinemann Ltd
Linacre House, Jordan Hill, Oxford OX2 8DP

⊖ A member of the Reed Elsevier Group

OXFORD   LONDON   BOSTON
MUNICH   NEW DELHI   SINGAPORE   SYDNEY
TOKYO   TORONTO   WELLINGTON

First published 1993

British Library Cataloguing in Publication Data
A catalogue record for this book is
available from the British Library

Library of Congress Cataloguing in Publication Data
A catalogue record for this book is
available from the Library of Congress

ISBN 0 240 51352 5

Page design, layout and typesetting by
A M Berkeley, Stevenage, England
Printed and bound in Great Britain

CONTENTS

Preface   *xiii*

Acknowledgements   *xvii*

1. BASIC LEGAL CONCEPTS   *1*

INTRODUCTION   *1*
What is 'Law'?   *1*
Law in the United Kingdom   *2*
Sources of Law   *3*
  Local Custom
  Common Law
  Equity
  Legislation
  Judicial Precedent
  European Community Law
Divisions of Law   *8*
The Burden of Proof   *9*
The Concept of Natural Justice   *10*

THE STRUCTURE OF THE COURTS   *10*
Criminal Courts   *11*
  Magistrates' Courts
  Crown Courts
Civil Courts   *13*
  County Courts
  Small Claims in the County Court
  The High Court

Appeals   *16*
    Appeals in the Criminal Courts
    Appeals in the Civil Courts

2. ESSENTIALS OF ENGLISH CONTRACT LAW   *18*

INTRODUCTION   *18*
  The Essence of a Valid, Legal Contract   *19*
    Offer and Acceptance
    Meeting of Minds
    Intention to Create Legal Relations
    Consent
    Capacity
    Consideration
    Legality
    Possibility
  Terms of a Contract   *23*
    Express and Implied Terms
    Conditions and Warranties
    Exemption Clauses
  Misrepresentation   *25*
    Fraudulent Misrepresentation
    Negligent Misrepresentation
    Innocent Misrepresentation
  Remedies   *26*
    Damages
    Rescission
    Specific Performance
    Injunction
  Other General Points of Contract Law   *29*
    Parties to a Contract: Who may Sue and be Sued?
    Quasi-Contract

3. CONTRACTUAL RELATIONSHIPS   *31*

THE PHOTOGRAPHER AS CUSTOMER   *31*
  Supply of Goods   *31*
    Merchantable Quality
    Correspond to Description Given
    Fitness for Purpose
    Guarantees
    Responsibility of Junior Staff
    Method of Purchase

Remedies
Supply of Services 34
Processing Laboratories - the Amateur Market
Processing Laboratories - the Professional Market
Servicing, Repair and Maintenance of Equipment

THE PROFESSIONAL PHOTOGRAPHER AS SUPPLIER 39
General 39
The Quality of Photography
The Social Photographer and Client 40
The Commercial Photographer and Client 42
The Editorial Photographer and Client 42
Speculative Submissions
Commissioned Assignments

CLUBS, SOCIETIES AND ASSOCIATIONS 44
The Contractual Relationship of Members 44
Advice and Guidance on Fees and Charges 45
Conciliation and Arbitration 46
Conciliation
Arbitration

4. EMPLOYMENT LAW 48

THE EMPLOYER/EMPLOYEE RELATIONSHIP 48
Employee or Self-Employed? 48
The Tests of Genuine Self-Employment
Contract of Service or Contract for Services
The Consequences of Employment or Self-Employment 50
Copyright
Tax and National Insurance
Employer's Liability
Contracts of Employment 51
Main Terms
Implied Terms - Employees
Terms in Restraint of Trade
Unfair Dismissal 53
Discrimination 54

HEALTH AND SAFETY 55
The Health and Safety at Work Act 1974 56
Application and Enforcement
Main Duties of Employers
Written Safety Policy

First Aid Facilities and the Reporting of Accidents
Duties of Employees
Criminal Offences
The Factories Act 1961   57
The Offices, Shops and Railway Premises Act 1963   58
The Fire Precautions Act 1971   58
Control of Substances Hazardous to Health   58

5. PHOTOGRAPHIC COPYRIGHT   60

COPYRIGHT LAW IN GENERAL   60
A Brief Overview   60
What is Copyright?
Why Copyright?
Copyright Law in the United Kingdom   61
The 1988 Copyright Act
Criminal Offence

PHOTOGRAPHIC COPYRIGHT IN MORE DETAIL   62
Copyright Protection   62
Definitions of 'Photograph' and 'Film'
A Photograph is 'an Artistic Work'
Live Events Including Wedding Groups and Other
        Poses - not Artistic Works
Originality
Passing Off
Restricted Acts, Infringements and Exceptions
Photography of Buildings, Sculptures and Other
        Three-Dimensional Works
Manipulation and Retouching
To Claim Copyright Protection
Ownership of Copyright   66
The 1988 Act - The General Rule
Employed Photographers
Students and Colleges
Ownership Under the 1956 Act
Duration of Copyright   68
Duration Under the 1988 Act
Duration Under the 1956 and 1911 Acts
Copyright: Assignment and Licences   69
Assignment of Copyright
Do I Need to Assign my Copyright?
Licences

Terms of Licences
Implied Licences
Copyright and Licence: Freehold and Leasehold
Moral Rights 72
The Right to be Identified as Author
The Right to Object to Derogatory Treatment
The Right Against False Attribution
A Client's Right to Privacy
The Effect of Death and Assignment on Moral Rights
Remedies for Infringement 74
Criminal Penalties
Civil Remedies
Ignorance is a Defence!
Whom to Sue
Copyright and the Moving Image 77
General
Rights of Other Artists
Ownership of Negatives and Other Materials 78
Negatives
Transparencies
Prints
Crown Copyright 80
International Aspects of Copyright Law 80
European Considerations 80

6. TORTS (CIVIL WRONGS) 82

GENERAL 82
What is a 'Tort'? 82
Damage and Liability 83
Liability
Liability for the Torts of Others
Remoteness of Damage
General Defences to Actions in Tort 85
Consent
Necessity
Self Defence
Statutory Authority
Justification
Mistake is no Defence
Remedies 88

SPECIFIC TORTS   88
  Negligence   88
    Contributory Negligence
    Remedies and Insurance
  Nuisance   90
    Public Nuisance and Private Nuisance
    Hounding by Photographer can be a Nuisance
    Remedies for Nuisance
  Trespass   91
    Three Types of Trespass
    Trespass to the Person
    Trespass to Land
    Photography on and of National Trust and Similar Property
    Trespass to Goods
    Additional Remedies
  Conversion   93
  Breach of Statutory Duty   93
  Libel and Slander   93
    Definitions and Distinctions
    Defences to Libel
    Justification
    Fair Comment
    Privilege
    Libel by Photography
  Model Releases   97
  Privacy Generally 98

7. LEGAL RESTRICTIONS ON PHOTOGRAPHY   99

OBSCENE AND INDECENT PHOTOGRAPHS   99
  The Obscene Publications Act 1959   99
  The Protection of Children Act 1978   100
  The Post Office Act 1953   101
PHOTOGRAPHY OF COURTS AND LEGAL PROCEEDINGS   101
  The Judicial Proceedings (Regulations and Reports) Act 1926   101
  Photography of Persons in Court   102
  Contempt of Court   102
    Pre-Trial Publicity
    Contempt of Court Act 1981
    Identity of an Accused Person
  Other Persons not to be Identified   104
    Identity of a Victim of Rape or Associated Offences

Identity of Juveniles
**PHOTOGRAPHY AT PUBLIC INCIDENTS
AND DEMONSTRATIONS**   *105*
   General   *105*
   Specific Offences   *105*
      Breach of the Peace
      Obstruction of a Police Officer
      Confiscation of Film or Camera
      Police Powers of Search and Seizure
WILDLIFE PHOTOGRAPHY   *107*
   Birds   *107*
   Other Species   *108*
   Plants   *108*

8. TRADING STATUS AND BUSINESS INSURANCE   *109*

TRADING STATUS   *109*
   Limited Company   *109*
      Limited Liability
      Insolvency
      Directors and Company Secretary
      Memorandum and Articles of Association
      Company Name
      Annual Audit, Accounts and Report
      Company Name on Stationery and at Premises
      So Why Start a Company?
   Self-Employed Sole Trader   *113*
   Partnership   *114*
BUSINESS INSURANCE   *115*
   Employer's Liability Insurance   *115*
   Public Liability Insurance   *116*
   Motor Insurance   *116*
   Professional Indemnity Insurance   *116*
   Libel Insurance   *117*
   Buildings and Contents Insurance   *117*
   All-Risks Insurance   *117*
   Insurance - Contracts of 'Utmost Good Faith'   *117*

9. THE NEW TECHNOLOGIES   *118*

LEGAL AND ETHICAL CONSIDERATIONS   *118*

Introduction   *118*
    Photography Defined
Misuses and Abuses   *119*
Copyright Considerations   *119*
    Manipulation and Moral Rights
Libel by Photography   *122*
The International Dimension   *123*
Conclusions   *124*

**APPENDIX 1
SAMPLE TERMS AND CONDITIONS OF BUSINESS
FOR WEDDING AND PORTRAIT PHOTOGRAPHY**   *125*

**APPENDIX 2
SAMPLE TERMS AND CONDITIONS OF BUSINESS FOR
 INDUSTRIAL AND COMMERCIAL PHOTOGRAPHIC STUDIOS**   *129*

**APPENDIX 3
SAMPLE TERMS AND CONDITIONS OF BUSINESS FOR
PROFESSIONAL PHOTOGRAPHIC LABORATORIES**   *135*

**APPENDIX 4
SAMPLE STAFF DISCIPLINARY
POLICY AND PROCEDURES**   *141*

**APPENDIX 5
USEFUL ADDRESSES**   *147*

PREFACE

For many thousands of people, photography is a living; for many hundreds of thousands (perhaps even millions), it is a loving. This book is intended for both: and for me, at different times of my life, photography has been both. I served for over ten years in the Royal Air Force Photographic Branch, and was fortunate enough to receive what I still consider to be the finest technical photographic training in the country at what was then the Royal Air Force (now the Joint Services) School of Photography at RAF Cosford. Many years later in life, having changed career direction totally after leaving the Services, and having gained a degree in law and some experience of business along the way, I spent four years at the head of the salaried staff of the British Institute of Professional Photography, for whose monthly journal, *The Photographer*, I now write as the freelance Associate Editor.

It is now nearly 30 years since I was first involved professionally within photography as a raw recruit at RAF Cosford. I would be lying if I said that I had enjoyed every minute of it, but much of it has been memorable: from climbing inside the wing of a V-bomber to photograph hairline cracks in the airframe, to sitting in the open door of a helicopter 10,000 feet over the China/Hong Kong border at the time of the Red Guards and the Cultural Revolution, monitoring the movements of Chinese troops; from climbing mountains along the same border with a pack mule and an 8"x7" format camera with a 200 feet film magazine and a 36 *inch* lens, to photographing the horrific aftermath of fatal air crashes; from covertly photographing extremist-fringe political gatherings to identify subversives and terrorists, to helping to locate the graves of the victims of the notorious Moors murderers using infra-red aerial photography; and from taking hours of cine film of radar screens (not the most exciting job I ever had) at the top of Penang Hill, to camping out in the woods in the north of Scotland to see if the Harrier jump-jets really could operate from hideaways instead of runways! Given the chance, I really don't think I would change any of it.

Whatever your particular involvement in photography, whether you do it to live or for love, you will want to ensure that you avoid the many legal pitfalls associated with your hobby or your business. And I hope that by writing this book I shall contribute something to photography, from which I have gained so much over the past three decades.

I hope very much that you will take the few hours necessary actually to read this book, rather than just dipping in to it or using it solely as a reference book. The fact is that much of what I have written is dependent upon having read related items elsewhere in the book. I have tried to avoid constant repetition, and so no part of the book is an independent, stand-alone section. So please read it through to give yourself some idea of what's here and what's not here, and then use it as a reference book thereafter.

It is also very important to look at this book in the proper perspective, and to see it for what it is. On a shelf in my study, I have a book on copyright alone that runs to 1,598 pages of very small and densely-packed type; it is nearly three inches thick, and it costs £125. I have another book, nearly two inches thick and comprising 721 pages, that deals only with copyright in sound recordings, film and video. And the *Copyright, Designs and Patents Act 1988* itself runs to 238 pages. That is why this book, in which the entire chapter on copyright runs to only 22 pages, is entitled *The Focal* **Guide** *to Photography and the Law*. It can be no more than that: a guide.

None the less, I hope and trust that it will be a useful guide, if only to alert you to those circumstances in which you might need further advice. I am aware that the law can be a very dry and sometimes daunting subject for the layman, but I have tried, throughout this book, to make it as user-friendly as possible. References to cases have been kept to an absolute minimum (although references to acts of parliament are more frequent), and I have studiously avoided using jargon and Latin terms: I am proud to say that you will not find one word of Latin anywhere in this book!

And to my female readers, a word of apology (or rather, of explanation): I am not a sexist nor a chauvinist, I promise you. Those who know me well will vouch for that. But rather than use he/she, his/her and him/her throughout the book (which makes for clumsy writing and difficult reading), I have used only the male pronouns. Indeed that is the convention used in acts of parliament too. It implies no insult, I assure you; and any reference in this book to the male pronouns must be interpreted as applying equally to both men and women (subject to the context, of course).

Finally, please understand the limitations of a book such as this, and please do not treat this book as if it were a definitive source of any aspect of the law relating to photography: it is not. Neither I nor the publisher accepts any responsibility for the consequences of any act or omission done or not done in pursuance of any advice given or not given in this book. The truth probably is that if you think you need further advice, then you almost certainly do; and that message will be repeated from time to time throughout the book.

ACKNOWLEDGEMENTS

I am most grateful to Margaret Riley, Commissioning Editor at Focal Press, for her kindness and friendship, for her enthusiasm for this project, and for her encouragement throughout its gestation. I am grateful, too, to my very good friend John Henshall FBIPP FRPS, with whom I had the privilege of working so closely during his tenure as President of the British Institute of Professional Photography. It was he who introduced me to Margaret Riley. And to my wife, Jenny, whose love and support I have had in all that I have done, my sincere and very special thanks for everything, not least for her meticulous attention to detail, both in the proof-reading and in the catering!

Notwithstanding the help and support I have had from others in the production of this book, any errors that remain are mine and mine alone.

AMB
June 1993

CHAPTER ONE

BASIC LEGAL CONCEPTS
A Brief Overview of the English Legal System

INTRODUCTION

The law as it relates to photography is only a very small, specialist area of the law. Or so you might think. But you would be wrong! Photography does not exist in a vacuum; it can not be cocooned or isolated from the society which it serves. Photography is an everyday part of everyday life, and the bulk of law relating to photography consists merely of the application of general law to the specific activity - photography. All photographers, whether amateur or professional, enter into contracts; photographers may be employed or may employ others; and all photographers, professional or not, owe the same duties to the rest of society as others do, and have the same rights in return.

You may want to know what rights you have if your local lab has ruined your film, what defences you have if your photograph is claimed to be libellous, whether or not you can lawfully take photographs on private property, or what to do if you think you have been unfairly dismissed. These are all matters of general law, not specific to photography: all of these questions - and more - are covered in this book.

Before progressing to particulars, however, it is as well to have a brief overview of the nature of law and of the structure of its administration.

What is 'Law'?

Attempts to answer that one, simple question have spawned countless volumes of legal philosophy and centuries of debate among legal theorists. For our purposes, all we need to say is that 'Law' is a body of rules and regulations applied with our consent and for the good order of society. In effect, law is an agreement among and between members of a society to enable that society to function. The society in question may be a club or association (where the 'laws' are more usually called 'rules'); it may be people coming together to play a game (yes, we can refer to the 'laws' of cricket, for example); or the society may be a nation state, or even two or more nation states agreeing together to an international treaty. For the most part, we shall be concerned with the law in the context of the nation state.

As you might expect, though, the definition given is a gross over-simplification. It is riddled with flaws, ambiguities and moot points. For example, '. . . with our consent . . .' implies a democracy of sorts and can not apply to a totalitarian state. Within a democracy, the imposition of a law against the general will of the people robs that law of one of its essential characteristics - enforceability! The recent experience of the Community Charge (Poll Tax) legislation is a good example. Also within our simple definition, reference to law being '. . . for the good order of society' is true, but it is not the whole truth. Law also has a role in protecting the vulnerable in society from harm and exploitation by others (which may or may not have anything to do with 'good order'). Some would go further, and say that law has a duty to protect people from themselves, or even to impose moral standards on society.

An absolute definition, therefore, is not possible. There is the added difficulty of the different uses of the word 'law'. We refer both to 'law' and to 'a law', the former being a collective body of law(s), and the latter being a specific piece of law, as in 'There ought to be a law against it'.

Law in the United Kingdom

Just to add still further to our difficulties of definition, the United Kingdom, though a unitary nation state, actually comprises separate bodies of national law. There is the law of England and Wales (more usually known simply as English Law) and there is Scottish Law. The law in Northern Ireland is not part of either body of law, but, for our purposes, is mostly indistinguishable from English Law. Then there are those laws that are applicable throughout the United Kingdom, of which the *Copyright, Designs and Patents Act 1988* is a relevant example. UK-wide laws may emanate either from UK domestic legislation, enacted by the UK parliament at Westminster, or from the European Community, in the form either of EC legislation or of a binding judgement of the European Court. They form part of the body both of English Law and of Scottish Law.

This book concentrates throughout on English Law, although attention will be drawn to known differences between English Law and Scottish Law.

Sources of Law

Law applied in the English courts may derive from one of the following sources:

- Local Custom
- Common Law
- Equity
- Legislation
- Judicial Precedent
- European Community Law

Local Custom

Given that English Law has developed by way of evolution rather than revolution, history has necessarily been a significant influence. Although it is now the least important of the modern sources of English Law, the courts have upheld local custom as a valid source of law, even in this century. An example would be rights of way over common land. To be upheld, the custom must be shown to have existed 'since time immemorial'. This was arbitrarily fixed as the year 1189, the first year of the reign of Richard I. In practical terms, the existence of a custom is presumed if it can not be rebutted from within living memory.

Common Law

Like local custom, the common law is historically-based and evolutionary. Unlike local custom, though, the common law is a major and highly significant source of modern law. The common law is judge-made law, and is the basis of the whole of English contract law, the laws of torts (of which more later) and much of the criminal law. There is no act of parliament, for example, which specifies or defines murder as a crime. Parliament has legislated on defences to murder and on sentencing, but the actual crime of murder remains a common law crime. Likewise with contract law: parliament has legislated where it has thought that the common law needs amendment (for example, the *Misrepresentation Act 1967,* the *Unfair Contract Terms Act 1977* and the *Supply of Goods and Services Act 1982*), but the whole underlying basis and principles of English contract law are judge-made common law. As a consequence of the days of Empire, the common law system has been exported to (or imposed upon, depending on your viewpoint) the vast bulk of the English-speaking world, including the United States of America.

Equity

It is often said, with some degree of truth, that law and justice are not the same thing. That is not a new phenomenon. The common law, that paragon of pragmatic evolution, became, paradoxically, very rigid, hide-bound by its own rules, and unable in some cases to dispense 'justice' as distinct from the law. And so a new, parallel system of judge-made law evolved. This was known as 'Equity' and was administered by the Court of Chancery. In those days, the Lord Chancellor was the king's principal secretary of state and 'keeper of the king's conscience'. When subjects petitioned the king to complain of the inadequacies of the common law, or to seek some redress which the common law was unable to provide, the advice of the Lord Chancellor was sought. Eventually, of course, matters were routinely delegated to the Lord Chancellor, and so emerged the Court of Chancery and the system of Equity.

By way of example, the only remedy available under the common law for a breach of contract was damages (that is, a financial sum by way of compensation). The common law courts were unable to grant injunctions, or rescission of the contract, or even an order that the contract actually be performed (known as an 'order for specific performance'). Indeed that remains the case today. All of those alternative remedies are 'equitable' remedies. And equitable remedies are only discretionary; they are not available as of right. Whereas (to continue with the contract law example) an aggrieved party who proves a breach of contract is absolutely entitled to damages under the common law, the granting of any of the equitable remedies is entirely at the discretion of the court.

Common law and Equity are now administered by the same courts, and so the same judge can award both damages and equitable remedies. Inevitably, Equity gradually developed rules of its own, and is now as bound by rules and precedent as the common law. But there is a basic maxim, which still holds good today, that *'Where Equity and Law conflict, then Equity prevails'*. And, given that Equity is about fairness and justice, there is a golden rule that *'He who seeks Equity must do Equity'* (otherwise expressed as *'He who comes to Equity must come with clean hands'*).

Legislation

Legislation - also known as statute law - is probably what most lay people think of as law: specific duties or prohibitions laid down in an act of parliament. In British constitutional theory, parliament is supreme; it can make and unmake laws to any extent it wishes. It goes without saying, therefore, that an act of parliament is a superior form of law to any other. If parliament does not like an element of the common law, or disagrees with a judge's interpretation of a previous act of parliament, then parliament can enact new legislation to change it.

The constitutional theory of the supremacy of parliament, however, has the practical limitations of public opinion and political possibility. A clear majority of members of parliament voted for the Community Charge (Poll Tax) legislation; public opinion forced a reversal. And a clear majority also voted for the United Kingdom's entry into the Common Market (as we used to call it) and later for the Single European Act and (on Second Reading at least, at the time of writing) for the Maastricht Treaty. In theory, what parliament has enacted, parliament can repeal; but it is an arguable point whether it would be politically possible to pass an act ending our membership of the European Community. So perhaps an act of parliament is not actually superior to any other form of law because, by accepting our membership of the EC, we have also accepted that EC law takes precedence over conflicting UK law, and, if it is politically not possible to withdraw from EC membership, then we have thereby enshrined EC law as the supreme authority!

Legislation as a source of law actually comprises more than just acts of parliament. An act of parliament is known as 'primary' legislation (as is some EC law, which we shall come to later), but there is also a variety of 'secondary' or 'delegated' legislation. Secondary legislation includes Regulations (usually by way of a Statutory Instrument), Orders in Council and by-laws. Statutory Instruments, other Regulations, and by-laws can only be made under the authority of an act of parliament; on authority 'delegated' by parliament. Orders in Council are nominally made by the sovereign (sometimes without the specific authority of an act of parliament) but, in practice, are only made on the advice of a government minister, answerable to parliament. Effectively, therefore, parliament is the fount of all legislative authority in the United kingdom. Even when Northern Ireland had its own parliament at Stormont, it was subject to and subordinate to the UK parliament (which is why the UK parliament had the authority to suspend Stormont and impose direct rule on Northern Ireland). Likewise, when and if there are devolved assemblies in Scotland or Wales, they will owe their existence to, and be subordinate to, the UK parliament, as now with all levels of local government throughout the UK.

Judicial Precedent

The hierarchical structure of the courts and the need for some certainty and predictability within the law have led to the system, or doctrine, of judicial precedent. The concept of judicial precedent is that each level of court is bound by prior decisions of superior courts in similar cases. However, the lowest level of court capable of creating a binding precedent is the High Court. Magistrates, crown court judges and county court judges do not create binding precedents. So decisions of the House of Lords, as the highest appeal court, are binding throughout (though the House of Lords is not bound by its own previous decisions); decisions of the Court of Appeal are binding on the High Court downward; and decisions of the High Court are binding on crown courts, county courts and magistrates' courts. However, even if a particular decision of one court does not form a *binding* precedent on other courts, it may nonetheless amount to what is known as a *persuasive* precedent. For example, one High Court judge, though not bound by a decision of a brother High Court judge, may be 'persuaded' by it. Similarly, a decision of a Scottish court may constitute a persuasive precedent within English courts, and vice versa, as may decisions of commonwealth or United States courts.

In the present context of the sources of law, the concept of judicial precedent overlaps to some degree with the common law, equity and legislation. A binding decision of a court may be in the establishment of some new principle or rule of equity or the common law, or it may be in the interpretation of a particular provision of a statute. It is binding nonetheless, and, if it concerns a matter of public importance, it is likely to work its way up the ladder of appeal until a definitive ruling emerges from the House of Lords.

Significant cases in the High Court, the Court of Appeal and the House of Lords are recorded in what are known as Law Reports, now amounting to thousands of volumes and probably hundreds of millions of words! A report will go in to great details of the facts of a case, the legal arguments used, and the court's decision. It is only the actual, true reason for the decision (which is sometimes hard to find!) which forms the binding precedent; comments in the judgement which are merely peripheral or by the way may be used as persuasive precedents only.

The concept of judicial precedent is applied in cases where the facts and circumstances are similar to those in a case already decided. But since any two cases would rarely be identical, there is much scope for the imaginative and persuasive lawyer to argue that his present case is different from one particular precedent and more akin to another (more favourable!) precedent. This is known as 'distinguishing', and a judge may himself choose to distinguish one case from another in order to justify finding for one side or the other in a case in the interests of justice.

European Community Law
We have already seen that there is an arguable case that law emanating from the European Community is superior to domestic, UK law. There is also another fine academic point as to whether or not EC legislation is 'primary' or 'secondary'. The strict adherents to the supremacy of parliament argument would contend that EC legislation is only effective in the UK because of an act of the UK parliament, and that the UK parliament can repeal that act at any time, thereby rendering any EC legislation as merely 'secondary'. Those who take a more practical view, and accept that the supremacy of parliament exists in theory only, are effectively saying that EC legislation is 'primary'. However, these arguments are academic for our purposes: for so long as the UK remains in membership of the EC, then EC law *is* superior.

Again, we have an overlap in trying to categorise sources of law, for EC law is either legislative or it is in the form of judicial precedent, both of which we have already examined.

EC legislation takes two forms, and differs from UK legislation in that it does not emanate from the parliament. The literal meaning of the word 'parliament' is 'talking place', and that is precisely what the

European Parliament is - a talking shop. It has almost no powers at all when it comes to legislation. EC legislation is initiated by the Commission (the EC civil servants) and is eventually debated, amended and 'enacted' by the Council of Ministers (a body of twelve, comprising one government minister of each of the member states). Along the way, the European Parliament is merely 'consulted'.

EC legislation may be either a Directive or a Regulation. An EC Regulation is 'directly applicable', which means that it has immediate effect throughout the Community as soon as it is enacted. A Directive is not 'directly applicable' as it is actually a directive to the individual governments of the member states to introduce a particular provision by way of legislation in their own national parliaments. There is normally a deadline by which the provision has to be enacted in all twelve member states.

Judicial Precedent, so far as EC law is concerned, is the binding nature of decisions of the European Court (of Justice, to give it its full title). This relates only to interpretation of EC legislation and decisions on whether or not a particular aspect of domestic law conflicts with EC law. The European Court does not make 'common law' like the English courts.

The European Court is an institution of the European Community. It is concerned only with EC law, and must not be confused with the European Court of Human Rights, which exists to uphold and interpret the European Convention on Human Rights (which has nothing to do with the EC), and decisions of which are only advisory.

Divisions of Law

There are various 'divisions' of law, some of which are more meaningful for our purposes than others. Common divisions of law are:

* Criminal and Civil Law
* Public and Private Law
* Public International Law and Private International Law
* Substantive Law and Procedural Law
* Common Law and Statute Law

There are many other possible divisions of law, few of which perform any valuable function. We have already looked at common law and statute law under the heading of 'Sources of Law'.

The division between criminal law and civil law ought to be fairly obvious. The criminal law is that body of law which defines anti-social behaviour not tolerated by society as a whole and for which society applies a sanction. The task of enforcing the criminal law falls primarily, though not exclusively, to the police. Other agencies empowered to enforce aspects of the criminal law include Her Majesty's Customs and Excise, Inspectors of the Health and Safety Executive, local authority Trading Standards Officers, the Royal Society for the Protection of Birds (RSPB), and the Royal Society for the Prevention of Cruelty to Animals (RSPCA). Civil law defines various rights and duties which each of us owes, and is owed, as individual members of society, and includes, for example, the law of contract, the laws of libel and slander (defamation), property rights (including copyright), family law (adoption, guardianship, divorce) and the laws of succession (wills and intestacy). The essence of the distinction between criminal and civil law is that civil law breaches do not generally concern the state or society, and action is initiated by the private individual at private expense, whereas criminal proceedings are usually initiated by an agency acting on behalf of the whole of society, and are at public expense.

The above description of civil law also adequately describes private law as opposed to public law. Public law consists of administrative and constitutional law and, of course, criminal law.

Other divisions of law do not really warrant discussion in this book.

The Burden of Proof

The task of proving a case in an English court usually lies with the party bringing the case. That means the prosecution in criminal cases and the plaintiff in civil cases. In both cases, the party defending the action is known as the defendant (except that in matrimonial cases, the defendant is known as the respondent, and there may also be a co-respondent). There are two different levels of the burden of proof in English Law: one for civil cases, and one for criminal cases. In criminal cases, where a person's good name and reputation are at stake, and possibly his freedom (and in former days, his life), the prosecution has to prove the case 'beyond reasonable doubt'. A much lesser burden of proof is applied to civil actions, where a case has to be proved 'on the balance of probabilities'. As a numerical guide, 'beyond reasonable doubt' probably means 95-98% certain, whereas 'on the balance of probabilities' might mean only 51%, although you must bear in mind that court actions are not scientifically predictable and nor are they mathematical games of chance!

When an appeal is made to a higher court, the burden of proof is on the party bringing the appeal, known as the appellant; the other party is known as the respondent.

The Concept of Natural Justice

The concept of natural justice, though not written in to any statutory provision, is scrupulously applied throughout the English legal system. This extends all the way down to the actions of private clubs and societies and disciplinary hearings of employers and professional bodies.

The basic rules of natural justice are that:

1. a person shall be informed of any charges against him;
2. that he shall have an opportunity to speak in his own defence; and
3. that no person shall be a judge in his own cause (that is to say, a 'judge' - which in this context means any person chairing or taking part in a hearing of any sort - shall be wholly impartial).

THE STRUCTURE OF THE COURTS

There is a broad division of the courts in England and Wales between those that administer the civil law and those that administer the criminal law. For our purposes, we really need only look at the County Courts and the High Court so far as civil courts are concerned, and with Magistrates' Courts and the Crown Court in relation to the criminal courts. There is a wide range of other specialist courts that need not concern us.

We shall also look briefly at the appeal courts: the Court of Appeal and the House of Lords.

But why should a book about the law relating to photography concern itself with the criminal law and the criminal courts? Well, breach of copyright in the course of trade or business is a criminal offence; so is disturbing (perhaps by photographing) certain wildlife in their natural habitats; and what about obscene publications? And taking indecent photographs of children? And at the workplace, the *Health and Safety at Work Act 1974* (and various regulations made thereunder) create a number of criminal offences for both employers and employees! And the

Companies Act alone creates over 100 criminal offences for unwary directors and company secretaries! Whilst we cannot look at all of the criminal offences you might commit in the course of practising your photography (whether as a professional or as an amateur), it is as well that you should have at least a basic understanding (and it will be no more than that) of the structures and procedures of the administration of the criminal justice system.

Criminal Courts

Magistrates' Courts

With the exception of trials by court martial (which need not concern us) all criminal cases in England and Wales come first before a Magistrates' Court; and about 95% of cases are concluded in the Magistrates' Courts too. Magistrates' Courts are manned by part-time, lay people (known as magistrates, or JPs - Justices of the Peace) appointed by the Lord Chancellor. In some metropolitan areas, however, where the case load for the Magistrates' Courts is particularly onerous, Magistrates' Courts are manned by professional, salaried, legally-qualified magistrates. These people are known as 'stipendiary magistrates'. Stipendiary magistrates generally sit alone to hear cases, whereas lay magistrates usually sit in threes. Lay magistrates are advised on matters of the law by a Clerk, who is salaried and legally qualified.

The very serious criminal charges, such as murder, treason, rape, and manslaughter for example (and there are others), have to be heard by a Crown Court, but even in these cases, the preliminaries are always conducted before the Magistrates' Courts. The magistrates will hear an outline of the prosecution case and decide if there is a case to answer. If so, the defendant will be committed for trial at the Crown Court. These hearings before magistrates are known as 'committal proceedings'. Magistrates will also determine whether the defendant will be held in custody pending his trial at Crown Court, or whether bail will be allowed and, if so, on what terms.

Lower down the seriousness scale of alleged offences (for example, a minor theft), the defendant has the right to choose to be tried either by the magistrates or before a judge and jury at the Crown Court. Below this, there is a whole variety of offences that are always tried before magistrates, and for which the defendant has no right to opt for a Crown Court trial. In actual caseload terms, most of these are motoring offences.

Magistrates may impose fines (within a fairly modest limit) and may pass sentences of imprisonment of up to six months. If the magistrates, having heard a case and convicted the defendant (or if the defendant has pleaded guilty), feel that the limit of their sentencing powers is insufficient in a particular case, then the magistrates may refer the case to the Crown Court for sentencing. (It ought to go without saying, of course, that this only applies in a case where the offence itself carries a maximum possible sentence that is beyond the scope of magistrates to impose.)

There are rights of appeal against the findings and sentences of Magistrates' Courts, and these are outlined later under *Appeals.*

Although we are looking at Magistrates' Courts in the context of the administration of the criminal law, magistrates do have certain civil court functions, notably in licensing and certain family matters (such as custody and maintenance). The vast bulk of the work of Magistrates' Courts, however, is in criminal matters, and, as we have seen, the overwhelming majority of criminal court casework falls to the Magistrates' Courts.

Any party to a case in the Magistrates' Court may represent himself, or he may be represented by either a solicitor or a barrister.

Crown Courts

The Crown Courts were established in England and Wales in 1972, to supersede what older readers will remember as the Assizes and the Quarter Sessions. The introduction of Crown Courts modernised the administration of criminal justice.

The Crown Courts have three primary functions:

1. to conduct original trials of defendants 'committed for trial' by Magistrates' Courts;
2. to sentence convicted offenders referred by the Magistrates' Courts in cases where the magistrates are of the opinion that their own sentencing powers are insufficient; and
3. to hear appeals from the Magistrates' Courts (but only against sentence or against conviction on the facts of the case; appeals on points of law lie to a division of the High Court). (See later under *Appeals.*)

When hearing an original trial of an accused person, the Crown Court comprises a judge and a jury. When the Crown Court is sentencing in a case referred by the Magistrates' Court, or when it is hearing an appeal, there is no jury, but the judge will usually be accompanied by two lay magistrates.

There are three different 'ranks' of Crown Court judge. More serious cases must be tried before a High Court judge (but the Crown Court is still the Crown Court; it does not become the High Court merely because a High Court judge is presiding). Below the High Court judge is the Circuit judge, so called because he is a professional judge assigned to a geographical 'circuit' (for example, the Midlands Circuit). Circuit judges also preside in the County Courts (civil courts) within the 'circuit'. And then there is the group of part-time judges known as 'Recorders'. A Recorder is an experienced, practising lawyer (usually a barrister, but sometimes a solicitor) who gives up some of his private practice time to sit in the Crown Court.

A High Court judge is known as 'Mr Justice *Surname*', and, whether sitting in a civil court or in the Crown Court, is addressed in court as 'My Lord' and referred to as 'His Lordship'. A Circuit judge is referred to as 'His (or Her) Honour Judge *Surname*', and is addressed in court as 'Your Honour'.

A defendant may represent himself in the Crown Court or he may be represented by a barrister. At present, solicitors have no right to present cases in the Crown Court.

The right of appeal from the Crown Court usually lies to the Court of Appeal.

Civil Courts

County Courts

As with the Magistrates' Courts in criminal cases, the County Courts in civil matters deal with the overwhelming majority of cases in England and Wales; something over 90%. Whether or not a County Court has jurisdiction in a particular case depends on the amount of the claim. Until quite recently, County Courts were only able to deal with claims amounting to £5,000 or less in contract or tort cases (except defamation - libel and slander), or £30,000 in some cases of trusts and wills. Now, however, in an attempt to clear a backlog of cases awaiting trial in the High Court, and to speed up the administration of justice, the scope of County Court jurisdiction has been increased dramatically to £50,000. So the proportion of the total civil cases being heard in the County Courts is likely to rise considerably from the present 90%-or-so. (Libel and slander cases are dealt with in the High Court because, unusually for civil cases, they are tried before judge and jury. Most civil cases are tried before a judge alone.) And unlike the case of the criminal courts, civil cases destined for the higher court (because the amount of the claim is above the County Court limit) do not have to be initiated in the lower court first.

The County Courts are staffed by Circuit judges, who sit alone and without juries. The general administration of the court is overseen by the Registrar, who will also adjudicate himself in small claims cases. The Registrar is always a solicitor of some years' standing.

Initiation of an action in the County Court is by way of a 'summons'. The summons outlines the plaintiff's case and the remedy that he is seeking. The summons is served on the defendant, who then has a short, fixed time (usually 14 days) in which to respond. The defendant may admit the plaintiff's claim in full, admit the plaintiff's claim only in part and contest the remaining part of the claim, or he may contest the whole of the claim. If the defendant denies or contests the plaintiff's claim, either wholly or in part, the defendant has to file a defence. He may also submit a counter claim against the plaintiff. If the defendant admits the plaintiff's claim, or if he fails to respond to the summons or to file a defence, then judgement may be entered against the defendant and in favour of the plaintiff. It is then up to the plaintiff to take further steps, if necessary, to 'enforce' the judgement. If, however, the defendant denies the claim and/or makes a counter claim against the plaintiff, then it will be necessary for the matter to proceed to a hearing, probably before the Registrar.

When the plaintiff files the original paperwork making the claim, he will have to pay a court fee. The fee varies with the amount of the claim. When and if the plaintiff eventually gets judgement entered in his favour, the amount of the court fee will be added to the amount that the defendant has to pay, so that the fee is (theoretically, at least) recoverable from the defendant, just as if it formed part of the original claim. If a case is disputed and proceeds to a hearing, the Registrar (or the judge, as the case may be) will usually make an order as to which side pays what amount of the costs.

It may be inferred from the foregoing that obtaining judgement in a case is not the end of the matter! Regrettably, that is so; and a 'victory' may be only a Pyrrhic or moral victory. Unless you are prepared to pay to make a point of principle, there is really no sense in commencing litigation against someone, perhaps a client, who is unemployed, or otherwise living on a modest income, and who has few or no assets. Similarly, you will be throwing good money after bad if you sue a company that is on the verge of liquidation. If the other party is unable to pay, then you will have lost not only the amount of the original claim, but also the court fees and (if you use a solicitor) your solicitor's fees too. (Your solicitor, of course, should foresee this possibility and advise you accordingly.)

Small Claims in the County Court
In order to reduce costs and to speed up the administration of justice, there are special provisions in the County Courts for pursuing small claims. The ceiling on what amounts to a small claim is raised from time to time, and currently it stands at £1,000 .

The small claims procedures are intended to be fairly simple and informal, and to operate without lawyers. You may still use a solicitor if you prefer, but, even if you win the case, you will not be able to claim reimbursement of your solicitor's fees from the other side. Because the amounts involved in small claims cases are, by definition, small, it becomes not cost-effective to use a solicitor, as his fee will almost invariably be greater than the sum in dispute.

County Court staff are usually very helpful, and are well used to assisting parties involved in small claims cases, many of whom will have had no previous experience of the courts or the law. The Lord Chancellor's Department publishes a number of guidance booklets to help potential litigants through the small claims procedures. They include the following, and they are all available from any local County Court:

*   *'What is a Small Claim?'*
*   *'How do I make a Small Claim in the County Court?'*
*   *'No Reply to my Summons - What should I do?'* and
*   *'The Defendant Admits my Claim - What must I do?'*

Alternatively, you can obtain the publications, and further advice, from the Lord Chancellor's Office (telephone 071 210 8500) or from your local Citizens' Advice Bureau.

The High Court
It follows from the foregoing that a civil case in which the claim exceeds £50,000, or that is an allegation of libel or slander, is heard in the High Court. The High Court comprises three divisions: the Queen's Bench Division, the Chancery Division and the Family Division. The Queen's Bench Division handles most matters that are of concern to us in this

book, such as contractual matters, torts (including negligence and libel), and breaches of copyright.

The main differences between civil cases in the High Court and those in the County Courts, apart from the 'values' of the claims heard, concern procedures and terminology, and cost. First, High Court civil proceedings are initiated by the service of a writ (as opposed to a summons in the County Court). Secondly, though a solicitor may represent you in the County Court, solicitors do not yet have the right to represent clients in the High Court, so unless you intend to do it all yourself, you will need a barrister. Almost certainly, your barrister will be involved at an early stage, giving advice on the merits of the case, both in terms of the law and of the practicalities of proceeding, and it will probably be your barrister who actually drafts the writ. And remember that you cannot have a barrister without also having a solicitor; you must have both. It is easy to see, therefore, how costs can quickly escalate as soon as you are involved in High Court litigation! And remember, too, that, should you reach an out-of-court settlement prior to the matter coming to trial, or, worse still, should you proceed to trial and lose your case in court, you will almost certainly end up picking up the tab for all or part of the legal costs, possibly including those of your opponent. Your solicitor's time, your barrister's time, the judge's time, the court's time, and the expenses of witnesses (and of a jury in defamation cases) do not come cheap! And if you or your opponent should engage a QC (Queen's Counsel - a particularly senior and experienced barrister), then you will be paying for at least two barristers on one side (for QCs always engage junior barristers to assist them). If all of this tempts you to think that you might present your own case in the High Court, remember the wise old saying that an advocate who represents himself has a fool for a client!

The Employment Appeals Tribunal, which hears appeals from Industrial Tribunals, is also a part of the High Court.

Appeals

Appeals in the Criminal Courts
We have already seen that an appeal from the Magistrates' Courts may be made to the Crown Court if it is an appeal against sentence or an appeal against conviction (not on a point of law). The appeal will be heard by a judge, probably accompanied by two lay magistrates.

Appeal from a Magistrates' Court on a point of law is to what is known as the Divisional Court of the Queen's Bench Division (which, you will recall, is part of the High Court). The Divisional Court will consist of at least two, and usually three, judges, and their decisions need not be unanimous. The head of the Divisional Court (and, indeed, of the whole of the Queen's Bench Division) is the Lord Chief Justice.

Appeals from the Crown Courts are heard by the criminal division of the Court of Appeal, although the Divisional Court of the Queen's Bench Division does has certain powers over matters of procedure in the Crown Courts.

The Court of Appeal is one stage higher than the High Court in the hierarchy of English courts, and judges of the Court of Appeal are known as the Lords Justices of Appeal; individually, they are styled 'Lord Justice *Surname*' (even if the judge is a female - as in the case of Lord Justice *(Elizabeth)* Butler-Sloss!). And confusingly, the Lords Justices are not the Law Lords; they are not even members of the House of Lords (unless an individual Lord Justice happens to be a peer in his own right).

In the case of a convicted person wishing to appeal on a point of law, then the right to appeal is absolute. But if the appeal is to be based on a point of fact, or is an appeal against sentence, then the authority either of the trial judge or of the Court of Appeal itself is necessary; this is known as being given 'leave' to appeal.

In certain circumstances, a further appeal, against a decision of the Court of Appeal, may be made to the House of Lords. (See below, at the end of the following section *Appeals in the Civil Courts*.)

Appeals in the Civil Courts
The civil division of the Court of Appeal is headed by the Master of the Rolls. The Court usually comprises three judges (Lords Justices), and, as with the Divisional Court, their decisions may be by majority. The Court hears appeals from both the High Court and from the County Courts.

Beyond the Court of Appeal, and at the pinnacle of the English legal system, is the House of Lords. The judicial members of the House of Lords are known as the Lords of Appeal in Ordinary: these are the 'Law Lords'. Note that a Law Lord is known as 'Lord *Name*', not 'Lord Justice *Name*', the latter being the style of address of judges of the Court of Appeal.

Leave to appeal to the House of Lords is normally only granted in cases where there is a point of law of general public importance to be determined. Usually five Law Lords sit to hear a case, and, again, a majority decision may be given.

CHAPTER TWO

ESSENTIALS OF ENGLISH CONTRACT LAW

INTRODUCTION

In English law, a contract does not have to be signed and witnessed; it does not even have to be in writing. There are certain limited exceptions to that sweeping statement, some of which are relevant to photography (for example, an assignment of copyright must be in writing and signed). There are tens of millions - probably hundreds of millions - of contracts entered into every day in Britain. Each of us makes maybe half a dozen contracts each day. When you buy your newspaper, there is a legal contract between you and the newsagent; when you go to the hairdresser, there is a legal contract between you and your hairdresser; and when you take your seat in a restaurant and order a meal, that brings into being a legal contract between you and the restaurateur. The list could be endless, of course; the point is that so many mundane, everyday activities give rise to legal rights and obligations and can have legal consequences if those rights and obligations are not honoured.

We shall see later how those legal rights, obligations and consequences might arise under other areas of law too, notably the laws of tort (civil wrongs); but for now, we are concerned with the law of contract.

In Chapter 1, we saw that English contract law evolved as common law, or judge-made law, with occasional interventions by parliament to enact statutes (acts of parliament) to override or supplement the common law, whether to correct injustices, to take account of changing commercial practices or technology, or to reflect the prevailing political climate (most consumer protection legislation, for example, has been enacted under Labour governments). That two-pronged evolution of the law - case law and legislation - will continue, but English contract law is now highly developed, with a vast mass of case law, precedent and statutes.

The Essence of a Valid, Legal Contract

For a contract to be valid and enforceable, the following essential characteristics must be present:

- an *offer* by one party and an *acceptance* by another party;
- a genuine *meeting of minds* between the parties;
- an *intention to create legal relations*;
- true *consent*;
- legal *capacity*;
- valuable *consideration*;
- *legality* of purpose; and
- the *possibility* of performance.

Let us briefly look in turn at each of these vital characteristics of a valid and enforceable contract.

Offer and Acceptance

There must be an offer by one party and an *unconditional* acceptance of that offer by the other. A *conditional* acceptance is not an acceptance at all; it is merely a counter offer. There can be numerous counter offers by both parties; this is the essence of commercial negotiation. A contract does not come into being until there has been an unconditional acceptance of the final counter offer.

An offer may be made in writing or orally or it may be implied from the conduct of the offering party. Display of goods for sale in a shop does not constitute an offer to sell: the offer is made by the customer who offers to buy. So to take goods to the checkout desk in a supermarket and hand them to the operator is an implied offer (an offer by way of conduct) on the part of the customer to buy those goods. The retailer is under no obligation to sell them. The contract is accepted by the retailer when the checkout operator rings up the price on the till. This particular aspect of contract law was interestingly applied in a criminal case *(Fisher v Bell)* in 1960. A shopkeeper was criminally charged with offering for sale a flick-knife contrary to the *Restriction of Offensive Weapons Act 1959*. He was acquitted on the grounds that to display an article in a shop, even with the intention to sell it, did not amount to an 'offer for sale'. Parliament quickly amended the law so that 'to expose or have in one's possession for the purposes of sale' became the offence, not 'to offer for sale'.

So, if an article for sale in a shop mistakenly has the wrong price ticket on it (say a camera marked at £12 instead of £120), the shopkeeper is not bound, *under contract law*, to sell it to you at the lower price. He can reject your offer to buy. (However, it is an offence under the *Trade Descriptions Act 1968* for a retailer to charge a price other than the price displayed. But, as the maximum penalty is only a small fine, the retailer may prefer to run the risk of prosecution if the discrepancy is significant.)

It is important to distinguish between what is an offer and what is an invitation to make offers. We have already seen that the retailer displaying goods for sale in a shop is inviting prospective purchasers to make offers to buy. The same applies at an auction. The auctioneer is not offering to sell; he is inviting offers: and he accepts an offer with the fall of the hammer.

An offer may be made generally to the populace at large (for example, a newspaper ad offering a reward for the return of stolen camera equipment), or it may be specific to a group of people or an individual. An offer becomes effective when it is communicated to the offeree. A person cannot accept an offer of which he is unaware. So, to continue with the reward example, the good citizen who returns your stolen camera equipment will have no legal, contractual right to claim the reward if he had not seen the newspaper ad and was totally unaware of the reward on offer.

An acceptance, on the other hand, is valid at the moment of acceptance. So if an offer is made by letter, it is not a valid offer until the letter is received, whereas acceptance by letter takes effect when the acceptance is posted. An offer may be revoked at any time prior to acceptance, but again, the revocation must be communicated to the offeree. As with an offer, an acceptance may be written, oral or by conduct, but acceptance may *not* be inferred from or imposed by silence. So to write to say that 'unless I hear from you to the contrary within seven days, I shall assume that you want ten mounted 20"x16"s' cannot, of itself, create a binding contract if the other party chooses not to reply.

These same rules on offer and acceptance apply too to more modern forms of communication. The basic rule that an offer must reach the offeree to be effective, but that the acceptance needs only to be sent (even if it never 'arrives') applies equally to telephone, telex, fax and modem communication.

One final point on offer and acceptance: an invitation to tender is an invitation to make offers; a tender is an offer, which will therefore be binding on you if accept.

Meeting of Minds

Although there needs to be a genuine 'meeting of minds' in order for there to be a valid and enforceable contract, this does not mean that the law will allow you to avoid a contract merely on the grounds of a simple mistake. If we agree that I shall buy your old camera for £50, and it turns out that the camera is a collector's item and probably worth nearer £500, then that is my good fortune and your bad fortune. You made a mistake, but the contract still stands in law. You and I agreed (our minds met) on the sale and purchase of *that* camera; its value is irrelevant. But if we agreed that I shall buy your camera, and you had in mind your Hasselblad and I had in mind your Nikon, then there is no 'meeting of minds' and so probably no enforceable contract.

The above examples are fairly black and white; in between are varying shades of grey. Whether or not there was actually a meeting of minds, or whether there was a mistake such as to render the contract void or unenforceable, is a question for decision on the particular facts of the case. There are ample decided cases by way of precedent or guidance, but they are far too numerous and detailed for a brief guide such as this.

Intention to Create Legal Relations

In law, a mere agreement is not necessarily a contract. The parties have to intend to create a legal relationship. So if I agree to meet you for dinner next Saturday and I fail to turn up, you can not sue me for breach of contract; there was no intention that the agreement (to meet for dinner) should create a legal relationship between us.

Within business dealings, there is always a presumption that legal relations were contemplated and intended, but this presumption can be rebutted. It used to be the case (possibly it still is) that football pools companies made a particular statement on their coupons to the effect that 'this agreement is binding in honour only', thereby rebutting the presumption of the intention to create legal relations. The bad news, therefore, if you think you might have won the pools, is that you cannot sue if the pools company fails to pay out; you must rely only on their honour! (*Jones v Vernons Pools Ltd [1938]* and *Appleson v Littlewoods Ltd [1939]* are the case-law precedents for this.)

However, there is a distinction to be drawn between stating that an agreement is 'binding in honour only' and a term seeking to exclude the jurisdiction of the courts. As a matter of public policy, a term within a contract which purports to exclude the jurisdiction of the courts will not be valid. Every individual has access to the courts to test his rights, and it is for the court itself to decide whether or not the case is actionable. So even in the 'binding in honour only' cases, an aggrieved party still has the right of access to the court, and it will be for the court to determine whether the agreement is indeed binding in honour only, or whether it is 'legally' binding.

Consent

Each party must consent freely to the contract and must not be induced into entering the contract by way of fraud, duress or undue influence.

Capacity

Each party must have the legal capacity to enter into the contract. Discussion on the capacity or otherwise of minors, the insane and drunks is beyond the scope of this book. So far as limited companies are concerned, any company has the legal capacity to enter into any contract provided it is so authorised by its own Memorandum of Association, which details, amongst other things, the objects for which the company exists. The objects clause will normally include a wide-ranging supplementary authorisation such as ' . and to do any other things incidental thereto which, in the opinion of the directors, are conducive to the business of the company'. Effectively, therefore, most companies have the legal capacity to enter into any normal business contract. If in doubt, ask to see a copy of the Memorandum of Association (which is a public document, a copy of which is lodged with Companies House).

Consideration

This is, effectively, the price that each party pays for the contract. In general, (though there are certain exceptions which need not concern us) there has to be something of value passing from each party to the contract. That 'something of value' may be money or money's worth, or it may be some act or forbearance to the detriment of one party and of benefit to the other. Consideration has to move both ways. Hence a promise to pay you £100 is just that - a bare promise; there is no consideration moving from you to me in return for the £100, and so there can be no contract. But if I promise to pay you £100 in return for your promise not to sell the copyright in your photographs to my nearby competitor on your retirement, then that is an enforceable contract; there is consideration moving both ways.

Consideration need not be adequate, and need not reflect the value of the consideration you are getting in return. If I choose to sell you my £7,000 car for only £700, then that is our business. A court will not concern itself with the inadequacy of the consideration. (Bear in mind, though, that such a transaction might amount to a gift for Capital Gains Tax or Inheritance Tax purposes; but that is outside the scope of contract law.) After the passing of the new copyright law (the *Copyright, Designs and Patents Act 1988*), a number of photographers received letters from advertising and PR agencies asking them to sign over all copyright in all future work carried out for that agency. Attached to the letters were £1 coins. Photographers were strongly advised by their various professional bodies to send back the £1 coins and not to sign over their copyright. Photographers who ignored that advice, pocketed the £1, and assigned their future copyright, will find themselves contractually bound by that. The £1 was good and 'valuable' consideration; the fact that it was wholly inadequate is irrelevant.

Legality
The purpose of the contract must itself be legal for the contract to be enforceable. If a photographer is 'contracted' by a client to take indecent pictures of a child, and the client subsequently fails to pay, then the photographer can not sue for his fees and charges. The purpose of the contract is itself unlawful (indeed criminal in this example), and so the contract is wholly unenforceable.

It is not only contracts to commit criminal offences which are unenforceable on the grounds of illegality. A contract to commit a tort (a civil wrong - for example, trespass) is also unenforceable, as is a contract against sexual morality. Prostitution, for instance, is neither a crime nor a civil wrong; but a contract with a prostitute will be illegal and unenforceable on the grounds of immorality.

Possibility
The law will not enforce a contract which is impossible to perform. Photographer, *P*, is commissioned by magazine editor *E* to get some photographs next week of the wedding of celebrity *C*. Unbeknown to both *P* and *E*, *C* has already cancelled the wedding. The object of the 'contract' is therefore impossible to perform, and the contract is unenforceable.

Terms of a Contract

There are two basic classifications of the terms of a contract. First, there are 'express terms' and 'implied terms'; secondly, there are 'conditions' and 'warranties'.

Express and Implied Terms
Express terms are those terms which have been agreed between the parties. The law generally takes the view that parties to a contract are

free to agree to any terms they choose (subject to considerations of illegality already referred to). There are circumstances, however, when the law will 'imply' certain terms within a contract. Implied terms may arise out of custom and practice, either within a particular trade or industry or within past dealings between the parties to the contract. As an example of the former, a baker's dozen is 13 not 12. Of more relevance, though, is the latter case of past custom and practice between the parties. If a photographer has regularly used the same lab for some years, and has always had prints matt finished, then the photographer can not suddenly reject matt finished prints and say that he wanted gloss finish (unless, of course, he specifically ordered gloss finish on that occasion). The lab would be able to rely on an implied term that the photographer wanted matt finish..

Perhaps more importantly, statute imposes implied terms in some contracts, particularly in the field of consumer law. The *Sale of Goods Act 1979,* for example, imposes the implied terms that goods shall be of merchantable quality, fit for the purpose for which they are sold, and shall correspond with the description of them.

Conditions and Warranties

A 'condition' is an essential term which goes to the very heart of the contract, and breach of a condition by one party would entitle the other party to treat the contract as a whole as having been breached. A warranty on the other hand is a term that is peripheral or subsidiary to the main purpose of the contract. A breach of a warranty does not mean that the contract as a whole has been breached. For example, a client may order a wedding album and prints from you for delivery a week next Friday, and he gives you a cheque for the whole amount. On the agreed date, you telephone the client to tell him that there has been a delay; his order will not now be ready until the following Wednesday. A few minutes later your bank advises you that the customer's cheque has bounced. Your breach is one of warranty. You have provided the goods (or will have provided the goods) but have failed to deliver them on time. Your customer, however, has breached a fundamental condition of the contract: he has failed to pay you.

You can make any term of the contract into a 'condition' rather than a 'warranty' merely by making its importance plain at the outset. We have all heard the expression 'time is of the essence'; that is a way of saying that delivery time is essential and therefore a fundamental 'condition' of the contract. Ultimately, however, in the event of a dispute, it is for the court to decide which terms are conditions and which are warranties. The significance of the distinction between a condition and a warranty is in the remedy available to the innocent party in the event of a breach (see **Remedies** below).

Exemption Clauses
(Sometimes also known as 'exclusion clauses'). Any clause in a contract which seeks or purports to restrict a party's liability to breach of contract will only be valid if it passes the test of 'reasonableness'. The concept of 'reasonableness' occurs a lot in English Law, and derives from the impossibility of legislating for every conceivable (and sometimes *in*conceivable) circumstance. Over the decades (centuries even!), lawyers have earned a lot of money arguing about what is and what is not 'reasonable'; no doubt they will continue to do so! But back to exemption clauses: under the *Unfair Contract Terms Act 1977*, it is no longer possible to exclude liability for negligence resulting in death or personal injury. So far as negligence resulting in less disastrous effects is concerned, the test of 'reasonableness' will apply. And under the *Supply of Goods (Implied Terms) Act 1973* (now superseded by the *Sale of Goods Act 1979)* and the *Supply of Goods and Services Act 1982*, any attempts to avoid the terms implied by law referred to earlier (of merchantable quality and fitness for the purpose) are invalid so far as a *consumer* is concerned; in business to business dealings, they will be subject to the 'reasonableness' test.

Misrepresentation

A misrepresentation is an untrue statement of fact intended to induce, and which actually induces, a person into making a contract. Note that it must be a statement of fact and that the offended party must have relied upon it in deciding to enter the contract. The common law of misrepresentation was considerably amended and extended by the *Misrepresentation Act 1967*. Both now exist side-by-side, the common law aspects applying only to the extent that they were not altered by the Act. (The *Misrepresentation Act* applied only in England and Wales. However, there is also a *Misrepresentation (Northern Ireland) Act 1967*, which contains similar provisions to the England and Wales Act, and the law in Scotland is along the same lines.)

Misrepresentation may be 'fraudulent', 'negligent' or 'innocent', the importance of the distinction being mainly in the remedies available to the offended party. Fraudulent misrepresentation amounts to deliberate deceit or dishonesty (and also amounts to the tort of 'deceit' - a civil wrong outside of any contractual considerations). A negligent misrepresentation is one made carelessly or recklessly, but without dishonesty. An innocent misrepresentation is one made in an honest, albeit mistaken belief in its truth and accuracy.

Fraudulent Misrepresentation

If you are the victim of a fraudulent misrepresentation, you may repudiate the contract totally and refuse to fulfil your own obligations under the contract (and, if sued by the other party, you may plead fraudulent misrepresentation as a defence and file a counterclaim for damages). Or you may initiate a civil legal action yourself, suing for damages for deceit (a tort) or for rescission of the contract and/or damages (under contract law). You may also refer the matter to the police with a view to criminal proceedings against the other party for obtaining property or pecuniary advantage by deception (the *Theft Act 1968*).

Negligent Misrepresentation

In the case of negligent misrepresentation, you may sue for damages (either under the provisions of the *Misrepresentation Act 1967* or, in limited circumstances, for the common law tort of negligence) or you may seek to rescind the contract. In the case of rescission of the contract, you can either rescind or repudiate the contract yourself, and plead misrepresentation in defence if you are sued, or you may ask the court to make an order for rescission.

Innocent Misrepresentation

Except for the right to sue for damages for negligence, the remedies available to you in the case of innocent misrepresentation are the same as for negligent misrepresentation.

Remedies

The basic remedy available in the event of a breach of contract (whether a breach of warranty or a breach of a fundamental condition) is the award of damages. Damages are monetary compensation for the loss suffered, and are generally available as of right once the breach of contract has been proved. Other remedies, which are at the discretion of the court, include rescission, an injunction, and what is known as an order for specific performance. Additionally, if the breach is one of condition rather than merely of warranty, the offended party may treat the contract as at an end and refuse to perform his obligations any further.

Damages

The amount of damages awarded will normally be limited to the amount of actual loss, whether direct or consequential. Damages in respect of consequential losses will be limited to that which was reasonably foreseeable; that is, loss which arises as a natural consequence of the breach of contract. In other words, there is a line drawn beyond which losses can be said to be too remote, and not a natural consequence of the breach. By way of example, there has been a case (albeit at County Court level, and therefore not creating a binding precedent) where a photographer was ordered to pay in the region of £4,000 damages in respect of failed wedding photography. The bulk of the damages was to enable the wedding to be re-staged and re-photographed by another photographer. That 'consequential loss' could be said to be reasonably foreseeable and arising naturally from the failure of the original photographer. But if one of the wedding guests tripped over and suffered injury whilst attending the re-staged wedding, that would not be reasonably foreseeable. So, although it could be argued that the guest would not have suffered that injury if it had not been for the original failure and the need for a re-staged wedding, the injury is too 'remote' from the original breach of contract and does not flow naturally from it.

Sometimes, a contract specifically states the amount of damages payable in the event of a particular breach. Delivery notes used by photo libraries, for example, usually contain a clause which says that a given sum (say, £400) will be payable for each transparency damaged, lost, or not returned by a specified date. A specific sum like that is known as 'liquidated damages' and, if a court decides the sum to be onerous, it will be classified as a 'penalty clause' and therefore not enforceable. Most damages are 'unliquidated' (that is, not actually specified within the contract).

In some circumstances, a court will award only 'nominal' or 'contemptuous' damages. Nominal damages may be awarded where the plaintiff proves his case but has suffered no real loss. An award of contemptuous damages - which may be as low as one penny - recognises that the case has been technically proven, but effectively penalises the plaintiff for bringing a trivial, vexatious, or even malicious case to court.

Where a contract has been breached, and the offended party has repudiated the contract, the party in breach is still entitled to be paid for work done up to the point of breach or repudiation. If he is not paid, he is entitled to damages for the amount of work done. Let us take an example from employment law. You discover that someone you took on six months ago is moonlighting for a competitor. That is a clear and fundamental breach of his contract of employment, and you are fully entitled to repudiate it. He is paid monthly, and you fire him immediately, two weeks after his last payment. He is still entitled to be paid for the two weeks, and he may sue you for it (although you may counterclaim for damages for *his* breach of contract, perhaps balancing out his two weeks' pay, but you would need to show that you have suffered actual loss of that amount).

Rescission

As we have already noted, rescission is one of the discretionary remedies available. In effect, rescission is an annulment of the contract, and it will only be granted if it is possible to restore the parties to the position they were in before entering into the contract and if the party seeking rescission has not unduly delayed in taking legal action. (A delay in taking action is an indication that the offended party has actually affirmed or accepted the breach.)

In any case where you apply to the court for rescission of the contract on the grounds of misrepresentation (whether the misrepresentation was fraudulent, negligent or innocent), the court may substitute damages in lieu of rescission and declare the contract as still subsisting.

Specific Performance

An order for specific performance is another of the discretionary remedies available to the court. It amounts to an order to the party in breach to remedy his breach by performing his part of the contract. An order will not be granted in cases where the award of damages provides a satisfactory remedy, and nor will it be granted in cases of personal services. If you have a contract with a supplier to purchase a particular new camera, and for some reason he fails or is unable to supply it, then your most suitable remedy is monetary damages, not an order for specific performance. But if, say, the camera is rare or unique - perhaps an antique - then an order for specific performance, instructing the dealer to honour his part of the bargain, might be granted. The reason for the refusal of the courts to grant such orders for personal services is fairly obvious: there is no objective way of ensuring the adequate performance of personal services. If I book you to photograph my daughter's wedding, and you subsequently pull out of the agreement, a court will not order you to 'perform' your part of the contract, as the court is incapable of ensuring that you do it properly, without malice or without a grudge; my remedy is damages.

Injunction

Another of the discretionary remedies, the injunction is quite rare in contractual cases. An injunction is an order of the court to refrain from doing something. It can be used, therefore, to enforce negative duties under a contract. If you have supplied photographs to a publisher, for example, and you have asserted your moral rights under the *Copyright Act (see Chapter 5)* for your images not to be subjected to derogatory treatment, and you have reason to suspect that the publisher intends to publish your images manipulated to such a degree that it would reflect poorly on your professional reputation as a photographer, then you could seek an injunction to refrain any such publication.

Other General Points of Contract Law

Parties to a Contract: Who may Sue and be Sued?

It may seem obvious, but it is only the parties to a contract who may sue or be sued in relation to that contract. So if you are not paid for work done, you can not sue the ultimate user of your photography if you were commissioned by that user's advertising agency. Your contract is with the agency, not with the agency's client; and so it is the agency you must pursue. Likewise, a customer can not sue your lab for breach of contract if the lab ruins your films. The customer's contract is with you, not your lab; it is you he will sue. In the first example, the agency, in turn, will have redress against the client; and in the second, you, in turn, will have redress against the lab.

Quasi-Contract

Although, as we have seen, a contract needs the agreement of the parties and can not be imposed by silence, there are cases in which the law 'imposes' contractual obligations on a party even without his agreement. Such cases are known as 'quasi-contract' and include court judgements (fines, compensation awards, damages, maintenance payments, and orders for costs, for instance) and payments or over-payments made in error. You may not have 'agreed' to accept liability to pay court judgements, or to repay money paid to you in error, but the law imposes an obligation on you, by way of quasi-contract, to pay these sums.

And Finally . . .

Do not imagine that having read this brief chapter on the general concepts of English contract law that you are now an expert on the subject! We have hardly scratched the surface. There are volumes upon volumes upon volumes of case law, learned textbooks and acts of parliament of direct relevance to contract law. This book is intended only as a brief guide for laymen - so let's now move on to some of the everyday contractual relationships that affect those with an interest in photography. And remember, if you think you need further advice, then you almost certainly do!

CHAPTER THREE

CONTRACTUAL RELATIONSHIPS

THE PHOTOGRAPHER AS CUSTOMER

As we have seen, any 'agreement' that you enter into with a supplier is, in law, a contract. This applies whether you write out a specific purchase order, or if you just telephone an order to a regular supplier; (remember, a contract does not have to be in writing). All photographers, whether amateur or professional, enter into contracts with suppliers. These will be both contracts for the supply of goods (the purchase of equipment, film and materials), and contracts for the supply of services (lab services, equipment repair and maintenance). And your contracts with suppliers will not be limited to the supply of photographic goods and services: the same considerations apply to all commercial contracts, for example, your stationery supplies, letterhead printing, vehicle servicing and the like.

Supply of Goods

The *Sale of Goods Act* (as variously amended over the years since the first such Act was introduced at the end of the 19th century) provides certain protection for the purchasers of goods. Basically, this Act imposes the following implied conditions in any contract for the sale of goods:

1. that the goods are of merchantable quality;
2. that the goods correspond to any description given of them; and
3. that the goods are fit for the purpose(s) for which they are sold.

These conditions apply only if the seller is in business selling that particular line of goods. They would generally not apply, therefore, to purchases of second hand equipment from anyone other than a recognised dealer of second hand equipment (although it could be argued that an amateur photographer who buys second hand equipment from a professional photographer is entitled to rely on the three conditions). But where the conditions do apply, the seller can not avoid them by way of exclusion or exemption clauses.

Merchantable Quality

The condition that goods supplied are of merchantable quality has to be looked at in the context of the 'deal'. You will not be protected if any defect was specifically drawn to your attention, or if you were given the opportunity to examine the goods before purchase and such examination ought to have revealed the defect. 'Merchantable quality' is not limited to the practical functioning of the equipment; it would include, for example, a scratch or other blemish on a camera casing, and not just to the operation of the shutter, say, or fogging through the camera back. But even a cursory examination ought to reveal obvious, external defects such as scratches, so unless you are purchasing by telephone or mail order, it is unlikely that you would be able to claim that the goods were not of merchantable quality merely because of obvious blemishes.

So far as other, more hidden defects are concerned, then you will be expected to discover them 'within a reasonable time'. It is sensible, therefore, particularly when buying expensive equipment, to give it a thorough 'test drive' as soon as possible.

Price, too, can be a relevant factor in determining whether or not goods are of merchantable quality. If you buy discounted goods, clearance sale goods or shop-soiled goods, then the quality you have a right to expect may be lower. So goods which may not of merchantable quality at the full price of, say, £1,000, may nevertheless be of merchantable quality if bought for £650.

Correspond to Description Given

The implied term that goods must correspond to any description given of them applies equally to any description given in printed sales literature and to any description made orally by the salesman. If the blurb for your new 35mm SLR says that the camera comes with a 28-70mm $f2.8$ zoom lens, and the lens actually supplied is only 35-70mm $f3.5$, then clearly it does not correspond to the description given. And if the supplier cannot provide you with the stated lens, then you are entitled to a full cash refund. Likewise, if the salesman tells you that the computer you are thinking of buying has an 80 megabyte hard disk, but when you take it home and install it you discover that the hard disk is only 40 megabytes, it does not correspond to the description given, and you are entitled to a full cash refund. These examples are both of fairly major and significant 'failures' to correspond to the description given; but the liability of the supplier would extend down to much more minor examples too.

Fitness for Purpose

That goods are fit for the purposes for which they are sold is different from their not being of merchantable quality or not corresponding to the description given (although there can, of course, be some overlap). A camera with a scratched casing may not be of merchantable quality, but a scratched casing does not render the camera unfit for the purpose for which it was sold. A faulty shutter, however, will almost certainly mean that the camera is unfit for the purpose (and it would also mean it is not of merchantable quality). Alternatively, if you say to the salesman that, for the type of photography you do, you need a camera with manual override of certain automatic functions, and (without you changing your mind about your requirements) he pulls the wool over your eyes and fobs you off with a camera that does not have those facilities, then the camera is not fit for the purposes for which it is sold; (nor, incidentally, will it correspond to the description given, even though it may be - and probably is - of merchantable quality).

Guarantees

Most expensive equipment is now supplied with certain minimum guarantees given by the manufacturer (or importer or distributor). There are two important points to note about guarantees in this context. First, nothing in any guarantee can reduce, minimise or eliminate any of your statutory rights (the implied terms and the remedies) under the *Sale of Goods Act*. Secondly, your contract is with the seller, not with the manufacturer or distributor. If any of the implied terms is (are) breached, then it is a breach of contract by the seller, and it is against the seller that your contractual remedies lie. Do not let the seller avoid his responsibilities by saying that it is for you to take up with the manufacturer, or even that he will take it up with the manufacturer on your behalf. Your remedy is against your supplier, the seller; the seller has his own rights, in turn, against his own supplier.

Responsibility of Junior Staff

The responsibility not to give misleading advice to a purchaser (whether by way of breach of the implied terms or by way of other misrepresentation) applies equally to the proprietor or managing director and to the most junior, part-time sales assistant. That is to say, the proprietor or manager can not escape liability for any misleading statement merely by saying that it was only a junior staff member who could not have been expected to know any better! So far as the purchaser is concerned, he has the right to expect the seller either to know about the products being sold or to admit to not knowing.

Method of Purchase

Your rights as a purchaser are unaffected by the nature of your purchase agreement. That is, whether you buy by cash, credit card, credit sale agreement, or hire purchase, your minimum statutory rights are the same. (Actually, you have even greater protection if you buy with a credit card, as the law actually puts the credit card companies in the same position, so far as you are concerned, as the supplier. That means that if any of the implied terms is breached, you can claim your money back from the credit card company instead of the supplier - which may be of benefit if the supplier has gone out of business soon after your purchase. Additionally, some credit card companies include insurance of the goods for a limited period after purchases made using the card.)

Remedies

The main remedy available to you in the event of a breach of any of these three implied terms is to 'rescind' the contract. In effect, that means putting both you and the supplier back to the position you would have been in had you not entered into the contract. In practical terms, that means a full cash refund (and your returning the goods, of course). You do not have to accept substitute goods, and you do not have to accept a credit note.

If the supplier refuses to give you a full refund, then your alternative remedy is to sue for breach of contract on the grounds of breach of an implied term (or implied terms, plural, as the case may be). You will notice also that there may be considerable overlap between breach of these implied terms and 'misrepresentation' *(see Chapter 2)*. It may be appropriate, therefore, to add misrepresentation as an additional or alternative ground on which to sue (but remember that the misrepresentation must be one of fact, not opinion, and must actually have induced you into entering the contract).

Supply of Services

The *Supply of Goods and Services Act 1982* lays down three basic criteria for the supply of commercial services:

1. that the work will be carried out with due diligence and competence;

2. that (unless there is a specific agreement to the contrary) the work will be carried out within a reasonable time; and
3. that (where there is no specific agreement as to price) the price charged will be reasonable.

Once again, these three criteria take the form of implied terms in any contract for services. Whilst the criteria are fairly self-explanatory in terms of their meanings, the main difficulty revolves around the extent to which you might be compensated in the event of their breach (or in particular, the breach of the first of the three - that the work shall be carried out diligently and competently).

The problem is that the liability of the supplier of the service is limited to that amount of the client's loss that is 'reasonably foreseeable'. So if, for example, a photographic processing laboratory, through its own lack of competence and diligence, loses or totally ruins a photographer's film submitted for processing, clearly the lab would be liable to repay the photographer the cost of the film and of the processing (if pre-paid): that amount of loss is self-evidently 'reasonably foreseeable'. Any liability beyond this would almost certainly differ between the cases of an amateur photographer submitting a film to an 'amateur' processing lab, and a professional photographer using a 'professional' lab.

Processing Laboratories - the Amateur Market
Processing labs catering for the amateur market, whether high street outlets or mail order, almost invariably use 'disclaimers' seeking to limit their liability to the cost of a replacement film. Often, the lab will offer the client the opportunity to inform the lab in advance of any 'extra value' that the film(s) might have, and to pay a premium price for additional liability. The precise wording used by one mail order amateur processing lab is:

> We take every care with your order, but in the unlikely event of your film or negatives being lost or damaged, our liability is limited to a credit for your payment and a replacement film unless you request Additional Liability Service (details available from address below). Your statutory rights remain unaffected.

Other amateur D&P labs use similar wording.

It would be difficult for anyone using such a service, having had notice of the disclaimer, and having failed to advise the lab of any extra value of the film, to claim anything beyond the processing costs and the price of replacement film(s). However, if the lab had indeed been advised of the special value of a film, and particularly if it had taken a premium payment, then it is equally difficult to see how the lab could escape liability up to the stated special value, provided that the client could prove actual loss up to that amount. The proviso is important, because it is not the object of contractual damages to enrich a plaintiff; rather, the object is to compensate for actual financial loss. In other words, a client could not pick an arbitrary figure, say £2,000, and inform the lab that the film (maybe of fairly nondescript holiday 'snaps') is worth that amount, in the hope that the lab might ruin his film and be forced to pay out £2,000. English contract law is not a lottery!

Indeed, staying with the amateur for a while, it is most unlikely that an amateur photographer will be able to prove actual financial loss as a result of any lack of diligence on the part of the lab. There will be exceptions, of course. Perhaps the amateur is doing a bit of moonlighting as a 'professional'; perhaps he has made a special visit to Australia to see a granddaughter he had never met, and the photographs were to be a special memento of that visit; or perhaps proud parents had hired academic robes to photograph their son on his graduation day. In all of these cases there would be a provable financial loss, and, if the lab had been alerted beforehand to their special value, such loss would have been 'reasonably foreseeable' and probably, therefore, recoverable by way of damages.

The important point, therefore, when dealing with labs serving the amateur market, is to make sure that any special value is notified to the lab in advance, in as much detail as possible, and with as much justification for the value as possible. The lab will either ask for a premium payment or not, but either way, the lab will have been put on notice and cannot later claim that the loss was not reasonably foreseeable.

As an aside, the question of such premium payments is regarded by some as most unfair. What it amounts to is the client paying for a form of insurance to cover the supplier's possible negligence. There is a very valid argument for the supplier of the service to be responsible for his own insurance in these circumstances, but there is no legal compulsion on suppliers to carry this form of insurance. The client can, of course, refuse to pay the premium; equally, the lab can refuse to take the film if it considers the risk too high. In the end, the client is left with the options of paying the premium, shopping around for a lab that will take the film without demanding a premium, or accepting the risk of only minimal compensation in the event of loss or damage to the film.

Processing Laboratories - the Professional Market

All of the same legal considerations apply to the professional lab servicing the professional photographer client as to the D&P labs serving the amateur market. The difference, though, is that it would be a nonsense for the lab to claim that consequential loss, over and above the mere value of the film, was not 'reasonably foreseeable' in the case of the professional photographer. A professional lab that has served a professional photographer client for any length of time will almost certainly know the nature of the work that the photographer does. In most cases, therefore, the extent of the consequential loss to the photographer in the event of loss of, or damage to, the film(s) will be 'reasonably foreseeable'. It might be the cost of a day's shooting in the studio, for example, or the cost of restaging a wedding. There does come a point, though, even in these professional cases, where what is 'reasonably foreseeable' to the lab will fall short of the actual losses which a photographer might incur. And it is important to remember that the lab's liability is limited to losses 'reasonably foreseeable' *by the lab*.

The photographer might have had to hire in models or specialist equipment to do the job; maybe there was the hire of an aircraft for aerial photography; there might be the cost of special transportation arrangements to get items to be photographed to and from the studio; perhaps an ad agency's art director will need to spend another day in the studio for the re-shoot; special wedding guests may have flown in from abroad; the portrait sitter might have to take extra time away from work for a re-sit; and there will almost certainly be the loss of earning time for the photographer (if the subject of the photography is capable of being re-shot) and maybe an element of lost goodwill with his client(s). All of these factors can affect the photographer's actual loss, but not all of them may have been reasonably foreseeable by the lab, or not to the full extent of the loss.

So if a professional lab loses or ruins films of a professional photographer, and the loss or damage is due entirely to the lack of diligence on the part of the lab, and even though an element of consequential loss to the photographer was reasonably foreseeable by the lab, the photographer can still be left carrying part (perhaps a large part) of the risk. Moreover, the photographer is still liable to his own client for breach of contract; the fact that it may have been caused by the lab (or any other third party for that matter) is irrelevant. As a supplier of services himself, the photographer has a contract with his client; and as client himself, he has another contract with his lab; there is no contract between the photographer's client and the lab. The photographer is liable to his client, and it is up to the photographer to take up matters with the lab.

So how can the professional photographer protect himself in these circumstances? First, he can take out a policy of Professional Indemnity Insurance *(see Chapter 8)* so that his own liability to his client is covered even if he finds he cannot fully recover the loss from his lab. Secondly, the professional photographer can ensure that his lab knows in advance of any special circumstances that add particular extra value to any film submitted for processing (like hire of models and equipment, wedding guests travelling from afar, the photographer himself having travelled abroad to take the photographs, or any of the other factors mentioned earlier). In this way, the lab is put on notice of the special value and cannot later deny that such losses were 'reasonably foreseeable'.

Servicing, Repair and Maintenance of Equipment
The same considerations apply to the contractual responsibilities imposed upon the provider of equipment repair and maintenance services as apply to photographic laboratory services (above). That is to say, the three implied terms (relating to 'due diligence', time and price) apply, as does the concept of 'reasonable foreseeability'.

If you are an amateur photographer, then it is very unlikely that any great financial loss in the event of poor workmanship on the part of a camera service engineer will have been 'reasonably foreseeable' on his part. So if you are having your camera serviced or repaired with a specific future task in mind, you must make sure that the service engineer is suitably informed, preferably in writing, before he undertakes the work. Otherwise, his liability will probably be limited to a refund of his charges, plus the cost of film and processing after the service until such time as you discover the faulty workmanship. That would normally be limited to only one or two films unless, say, you immediately went away on holiday and exposed half-a-dozen rolls of film that were not processed until your return.

In the case of a professional photographer, then a degree of financial loss is more 'reasonably foreseeable' on the part of the service engineer (provided, of course, that he knows that you are professional). Even so, the service engineer still might not be liable for the whole of any losses you suffer. As a professional, you would be expected to anticipate occasional equipment failure and carry spare, serviceable equipment with you as back-up. If the fault is one that ought to be obvious to you while actually using the camera, then it is doubtful if the service engineer would be held liable for the whole of any losses you might suffer: he would argue that you should have used a spare. The situation would be different if the fault was one that was not apparent until the films had been processed. Even then, if the subject is one that is capable of being re-photographed, you would be expected to re-photograph it. It is a general principle of contract law that any 'injured' party is expected to 'mitigate' (minimise) his own losses as far as he reasonably can. Moreover, bear in mind that in cases of repair and maintenance, we are, by definition, talking about old (or at least 'used') equipment: the law would not expect used equipment, no matter how recently serviced or repaired, to function as though it were new. Probably, therefore, the degree of liability for faulty repair will be less than the degree of liability for the supply of new equipment that was faulty; and the degree of liability will be likely to diminish with the age and prior usage of the equipment.

Your contracts with service engineers will not be limited to repair and maintenance of your camera equipment. You will also have other photographic equipment (perhaps enlargers, processing machines and the like), photocopiers, typewriters, computers and other office equipment and, of course, motor vehicles. The same three basic implied terms apply to contracts for the repair, servicing and maintenance of all of these items as apply to your camera equipment, and the same concept of 'reasonable foreseeability' applies.

THE PROFESSIONAL PHOTOGRAPHER AS SUPPLIER

General

If you were to read through all of the foregoing part of this Chapter, outlining your rights when dealing with suppliers, and then put the boot on the other foot, so to speak, you will have a very good idea of the duties and liabilities that you, as a professional photographer, owe in turn to your clients. Your clients have the same rights when dealing with you as a supplier as you have in dealings with your own suppliers.

All professional photographers are suppliers of services, and so are fully bound by the provisions of the *Supply of Goods and Services Act*. Many professional photographers are also suppliers of goods (albums, mounts, frames and the like), thereby bringing them within scope of the *Sale of Goods Act* too. And remember that 'professional photographer' in this context means anyone offering and providing a photography service for reward: it is not limited to the established, full-time professional.

Although, as we have seen, various acts of parliament or considerations of public policy impose certain implied conditions in contracts or render certain contracts or conditions unenforceable, the basic rule is that parties to a contract are free to agree whatever terms they wish. And in the event of a dispute with a client, the first question that your solicitor, your professional association or a court will ask, and the first question that you should ask yourself, therefore, is: what was agreed? The terms of the agreement, whether in writing or not, are the terms of the contract. The agreed terms are the starting point for the resolution of any misunderstandings, and they are the starting point for assessing liability in the event of a dispute. It is worth repeating, therefore, that written agreements, or at least written confirmation of oral agreements (even if only in the form of file notes made at the time), make misunderstandings and disputes easier to resolve.

Copyright considerations of photographers' contracts with clients are dealt with in Chapter 5 (PHOTOGRAPHIC COPYRIGHT).

The Quality of Photography

You now know that one of the terms implied into any contract you have with a client is that you will perform the service with due diligence and competence *(Supply of Goods and Services Act)*. But photography, of course, is very subjective, and often there are complaints from clients about the 'quality' of photography when what they really mean is that they just don't like it.

Clearly, if a picture is out of focus, significantly over- or underexposed, or if the colour balance is wrong, then you will have failed to exercise due skill and competence. But even then, if your contract was to produce 24 pictures, and you produced 30 pictures, of which only six were 'faulty', then you have fully performed your part of the contract, and your client will have no comeback (other than to go elsewhere next time). However, if your client merely dislikes the lighting, composition or pose, then that in itself is not grounds for claiming breach of contract on your part, provided, of course, that you have exercised due diligence and competence reasonably expected of a professional, and have followed any specific instructions of the client.

The Social Photographer and Client

Wedding and portrait photographers deal in the main with end consumers rather than with corporate clients. That puts a special responsibility on social photographers, as their clients are often first-time purchasers of photography services, and possibly, therefore, naïve in business dealings in general or in photography specifically. This can be a relevant factor in the event of a dispute that reaches court, as the courts may, in certain circumstances, take into account the relative bargaining strengths of the parties to an agreement, and their relative expertise in the subject matter.

Clearly all of your business dealings should be above board and beyond reproach, but whereas you might assume certain knowledge and a degree of experience and expertise in your dealings with corporate clients, such an approach when dealing in the consumer market can be dangerous and expensive! It is vital, therefore, that details of all of your bookings and commissions are recorded in writing, preferably using standard terms and conditions of trading (amended in individual cases if and when necessary). Disputes, when they arise, are often based on simple misunderstandings, and frequently degenerate thereafter into seemingly irreconcilable differences, and ultimately, perhaps, to litigation. To minimise the risk of disputes and litigation, you should therefore seek to avoid misunderstandings. You should ensure that your terms and conditions (when completed with individual names, dates, times and any special requirements), are signed by your client as an acknowledgement not only of the agreement itself but also of the specific details. Do not rely only on oral agreements. This is so obvious in the case of wedding photography, and yet the number of wedding photographers who ignore it is quite staggering!

Remember that your client's contract is with you, not with the makers of your film or camera, and not with your lab. If you agree to photograph a wedding, then you are contractually bound to produce the photographs of that wedding, even if something goes terribly wrong that was not your fault and over which you had no control. If your camera fails, if your film is faulty, or if your lab ruins your film (to the extent that you are unable to supply any or all the photographs), it is you who are in breach of contract, not any of your suppliers. Your clients may be sympathetic; they may not. Ultimately, they have the right to sue for damages for breach of contract, and you will be liable for any consequential losses that were 'reasonably foreseeable'. That might entail restaging the wedding (including flowers, cake, hiring of cars, dresses and suits, and, of course, hiring another photographer!), perhaps with the cost of flying in important guests from abroad. Whether or not, and the extent to which, you might in turn have a valid claim against your suppliers, will depend upon the considerations outlined in the earlier part of this Chapter (THE PHOTOGRAPHER AS CUSTOMER). You would be well advised to consider a policy of Professional Indemnity Insurance to cover your liabilities in such circumstances.

When dealing with the general public as consumers (as opposed to business-to-business dealings), you must, if you are registered for Value Added Tax, ensure that all of your prices quoted and displayed are inclusive of VAT, or at least indicate clearly that they are subject to the addition of VAT.

The Commercial Photographer and Client

In this context, 'commercial photographer' does not necessarily mean one whose photography is what is usually classified as 'commercial photography': rather, it means any photographer working for a commercial client as opposed to a 'consumer' client, irrespective of the nature of the photography.

Unlike the photographer dealing with the consumer client, you do not need to quote VAT-inclusive prices to a business client (indeed it is normal practice not to). And in your dealings with your clients, you can reasonably expect them to have a degree of experience and expertise in business and, in many cases, in the actual commissioning and buying of photography. The relative bargaining positions between photographer and client are therefore more even than is the case with social photography (actually swinging very much in favour of the client in many cases).

As with the social photographer, your client's contract is with you, not with any of your suppliers. The same considerations apply, therefore, in respect of your liability in the event of film faults, equipment failure, and disasters at the lab. Professional Indemnity Insurance is therefore a must for the prudent commercial photographer too.

The 'contractual relationship' aspect applies both ways, of course. Much commercial photography is commissioned not by the end user, but by the end user's advertising or PR agency. In such cases, your contract is with the agency, not with the end user. The fact that the end user (the agent's client) might not like the photographs, or decides not to use them, or for whatever reason fails to pay the agency (a dispute, or cash flow problems perhaps, or even liquidation) is wholly irrelevant to the contract between you and the agency. If you have performed your part of the contract (on time and with due diligence and competence), then you are fully entitled to expect the agency to fulfil its part of the contract: to pay you!

The Editorial Photographer and Client

Most of the contractual aspects of the relationship between the freelance editorial photographer and his client will revolve around copyright and usage considerations (and payment, of course) for which see the Chapter on PHOTOGRAPHIC COPYRIGHT (Chapter 5). In the case of speculative submissions, these will be almost the only considerations.

However, in the event of commissioned editorial photography, you will also need to ensure that there is agreement as to out-of-pocket expenses, for example, and ownership of the materials (which is different from ownership of copyright).

Speculative Submissions

In the case of speculative submissions to newspapers and magazines, remember that you cannot simply impose a contract on another party by their saying or doing nothing. You cannot say in a covering letter, for example, that unless you hear to the contrary within a given time, you will assume that the pictures are accepted for publication. If you do not get your pictures back within a reasonable time, or even never, then you know not to submit to that publication again. Nor is there any obligation on the part of publisher to return your unwanted and unused submission by any given date, or, say, by registered post: you cannot impose any such conditions.

Moreover, many publications include printed notices to the effect that unsolicited submissions are sent entirely at the sender's own risk. That would not allow the magazine deliberately or recklessly to damage your submissions with impunity, but it will be very difficult for you to gain any recompense at all in the event of damage to your transparencies (in the case of prints, it really becomes irrelevant). Remember that you would have no contract with the publisher, and any action you take would have to be based on negligence rather than breach of contract. The publisher could probably rely on the disclaimer notice in all but the most exceptional of cases.

If your unsolicited work is actually published, or is accepted for publication, then a contract comes into being. If you have a history of previous dealings with that publication, then (unless anything to the contrary was agreed) the terms of any past dealings will be implied into the present contract. However, if your covering letter offered certain other terms for publication, and the picture(s) has (have) been published without any further reference to you, then technically your terms have been 'accepted'. This would apply whether or not you have worked previously for that same publisher.

In the total absence of any agreed terms, then you are entitled to 'reasonable' payment, probably based on accepted industry terms (perhaps NUJ rates, for example).

Commissioned Assignments

In the case of commissioned editorial photography, you are largely in the same position as any other photographer working for a commercial client (see *The Commercial Photographer and Client* above). You will have agreed a price with the commissioning editor, and (unless the agreement says otherwise) you are entitled to payment for the work once it has been delivered (or within the agreed time or a reasonable time thereafter) whether or not the pictures are published.

If you have agreed to limited usage rights, then your agreement with the commissioning editor should include a provision for the return of the pictures (perhaps specifically by registered post, at the highest compensation level) within a reasonable time after publication. And if the images are capable of further use elsewhere at a later stage, you should certainly include a term providing for the payment to you of a reasonable sum in the event of loss of, or damage to, the photographs while in the possession of the publication.

Sample Terms and Conditions of Business

Sample Terms and Conditions of Business for Wedding and Portrait Photography can be found in Appendix 1 (page 125); for Industrial and Commercial Photographic Studios in Appendix 2 (page 129); and for Professional Photographic Laboratories in Appendix 3 (page 135).

CLUBS, SOCIETIES AND ASSOCIATIONS

The Contractual Relationship of Members

A contract comes into being when you join a club, association or society. Effectively, you are entering a contract with all other members of that club, association or society to abide by its rules. By joining the club, you are agreeing to all of its rules.

Subject, where appropriate, to the various laws relating to charities or companies, any association (including anything from local camera clubs to large professional institutes) can make whatever rules it chooses. In the case of an association that is a company (for example, the British Institute of Professional Photography and the Professional Photographic Laboratories Association), the company's Articles of Association are its rules. In the case of a less formal association, the rules may be known simply as 'the Rules' or maybe as 'the Constitution'.

Whatever form they take, the rules will contain various provisions relating to the management of the organisation, including membership criteria, subscriptions, expulsion or suspension from membership, alteration of the rules, and procedures in the event of the association being wound up. And the rules will usually provide for some form of delegated authority, by which its Officers, Board or Executive Committee may make further regulations relating to the management of the association, but the rules themselves can usually only be altered by the association as a whole at a general meeting.

If you have a dispute with an association of which you are a member, and the dispute concerns the internal management and workings of the association, the courts will generally not intervene provided that the association has acted in accordance with its own rules and in accordance with the principles of natural justice *(see Chapter 1)*. Obviously, if you have a claim against the association that is not related to its own internal management and administration (for example if you are a supplier of services to the association on a commercial basis, or if the association has caused you damage or injury), then you can seek redress through the courts in the usual way.

Advice and Guidance on Fees and Charges

Do not expect your professional association or trade association to give advice and guidance on fees and charges, nor even on recommended Terms and Conditions of Business, as part of your benefits of membership. No doubt some associations give such advice, but it is actually unlawful for them to do so unless any such guidance or recommendation is registered with the Office of Fair Trading. The *Restrictive Trade Practices Act 1976* deems any advice or guidance given collectively by any association to its members, on any matter relating to the terms on which members carry on business, and no matter how informally or unofficially that advice may have been given, to be an instruction to all members to adhere to such advice or guidance. This amounts to a 'registerable agreement' under the Act; and a 'registerable agreement' has to be registered with the Director General of Fair Trading who has wide-ranging powers (and sometimes duties) to refer agreements to the Restrictive Practices Court (a part of the High Court).

Any advice given that constitutes a 'registerable agreement' and which is not in fact registered is unlawful; and the chances of obtaining registration for recommended terms and conditions of business, particularly if there is any advice on fees and charges, are almost nil. The reason for this is that such recommendations from associations are regarded as being anti-competitive in nature and against the public interest. In effect, the law presumes any association that advises its members on their terms and conditions of business to be operating a cartel, and, if the association nevertheless wishes to apply to register such an agreement, the onus is on the association to rebut the presumption and demonstrate that the agreement is in the public interest.

Conciliation and Arbitration

Many professional and trade associations offer conciliation services, and access to arbitration services, for members in dispute with their clients or with each other.

The words 'conciliation' and 'arbitration' are often used by those who know no better as though they are synonyms: they are not.

Conciliation

Conciliation is an informal attempt at mediation between two (or more) parties in dispute. Conciliation findings and recommendations are not binding on the parties, unless, of course, there is a contractual agreement between the parties to the contrary, in which case a party not accepting and acting upon the findings and recommendations will be in breach of contract.

Members of an association might find that they are contractually bound by the rules or Articles of Association of the particular association to accept the findings of any conciliation undertaken under the auspices of that association. In such cases, any contractual obligation will be to the association, and not to a third party client. A third party client will have no legal remedy for failure of an association member to adhere to the findings of any such conciliation, but might be able to put pressure on the association to take disciplinary action against the recalcitrant member (subject, of course, to the Rules or Articles of Association making provision for disciplinary actions). Further, a client may use the conciliation findings as evidence in his support in any subsequent legal action he might take against the member.

Arbitration

Arbitration, though informal by comparison to litigation in the courts, is more formal than conciliation in that the findings are binding on the parties.

Arbitration procedures are governed by the successive *Arbitrations Acts (1950, 1975* and *1979).* There are limited rights of appeal to the High Court on points of law, and, in the event of the losing party refusing or failing to carry out the terms of an arbitration award, an application may be made to the court to enforce the award, just as if it were a court judgement.

The Office of Fair Trading Code of Practice for the Photographic Industry obliges those photographic associations that are subscribers to the Code (which is most of them) to arrange arbitration hearings when requested to do so by dissatisfied consumers.

CHAPTER FOUR

EMPLOYMENT LAW

THE EMPLOYER/EMPLOYEE RELATIONSHIP

A judge once compared employing people to keeping lions. In fact, he suggested that the latter was probably a safer thing to do legally! To use an overworked metaphor, employment law truly is a minefield. It is a vast, specialist area of law with many nasty traps for the unwary. Not only are there the administrative (some would say 'bureaucratic') provisions relating to contracts of employment, unfair dismissal, redundancy, discrimination, industrial tribunals and the like, but there are also the questions of health and safety, an employer's liability for acts and omissions of his employees, and matters of industrial disputes and relationships with trades unions.

Generally speaking, industrial relations do not currently present a problem within photography; but that has not always been the case. Some readers will remember the violent mass picketing in the Grunwick processing labs dispute of the early 1970s. However, details of collective industrial and employment law, such as trades union recognition, industrial disputes, strike ballots and picketing, are beyond the scope of this book, and this section will concentrate only on employment law as it relates to individuals.

Employee or Self-Employed?

The status of anyone you engage (if you are the 'employer'), or the terms on which you are engaged (if you are the 'employee') are vital for at least three reasons. First, there are tax and national insurance implications; second, there are the general insurance and liability considerations;

and third (in photography and other creative fields) there is the matter of ownership of copyright.

Sham arrangements of bogus 'self-employment' are rife in some industries, most notably in building and construction. Copyright is not a consideration there, but the first two are. Many employers have had their fingers burned to the point, in some cases, of forced liquidation and personal bankruptcy. But these things always happen to some else, don't they? Maybe; but to someone else, you *are* someone else, and it could be your turn next!

The Tests of Genuine Self-Employment
Let's look at the series of 'tests' which the courts (and the Inland Revenue inspectors) use to determine whether someone is genuinely self-employed or not. Then we shall look at the consequences.

They will ask a number of questions, such as:

- Do you work for more than one 'employer'?
- Do you provide your own equipment and materials?
- Is your own capital at risk?
- Are you expected to put right any mistakes in your own time and at your own expense?
- Do you control not only what you do, but the way in which you do it?
- Can you engage someone else to deputise for you?
- Do you have a business address and proper business stationery?
- Are you registered for VAT?
- Do you submit invoices?

No single question or answer is definitive; each case is judged on its own circumstances (for example, VAT registration might not be appropriate). If you can truthfully answer 'yes' to each question, then you are probably self-employed. But if you answer 'no' to very many of these questions, then you are almost certainly an employee. And one factor that is specifically not taken into account is what the parties to the agreement themselves call the arrangement. If you engage someone, the fact that you might both agree that it will be on a 'self-employed' basis is wholly irrelevant. It is the tests that matter.

Contract of Service or Contract for Services

If you are genuinely self-employed, then your 'employer' is actually your client, and your relationship is one of a 'contract for services'. If you are an employee, then your relationship with your employer is one of a 'contract of service'. The distinction is crucial: a contract for services, or a contract of service.

The Consequences of Employment or Self-Employment

Copyright

We shall see later in the book that, unless validly assigned, copyright in any photograph belongs to the photographer, except in the case of a photograph taken by an employee in the course of his employment, in which case copyright belongs to the employer. The *Copyright, Designs and Patents Act 1988* defines 'employee' as one who is 'engaged under a contract of service'. The chances of a part-time wedding photographer 'employed' by a mainstream studio actually being legally an employee rather than self-employed are remote. He is probably engaged on a contract for services, not a contract of service. He therefore owns the copyright in any photographs he takes for you. (So make sure he signs something to the effect that his copyright in any photographs he takes when engaged by you is assigned to you absolutely. *See Chapter 5.*)

Tax and National Insurance

But what if you apply the above tests and decide that your part-time operator - or anyone else you engage for that matter - is really your employee after all? Have you been deducting PAYE and National Insurance payments from that person and passing them over to the Inland Revenue on a monthly basis? If the answer is 'no', the Inland Revenue can regard any payments that you have made to that person as being *net* payments, and can come to you, as the employer, to gross them up for tax and NI purposes. In other words, you are liable for any unpaid tax and NI, not the employee; and the Revenue can demand back payments from you for the last six years! There have been many such cases in recent years, and one small company, a family firm, was faced with a £70,000 demand. The company could not pay; the Revenue went to court to have the company wound up; the owner had given personal guarantees to his bank and ended up homeless and personally bankrupt.

Employer's Liability

Later in this book, we shall look in more detail at the general questions of liability for torts (civil wrongs). Meanwhile, it is worth noting here that an employer is liable for the negligence (and other torts) of his employees acting in the course of their employment and, indeed, for injuries caused *to* employees in the course of their employment and which arise from the employer's own negligence or breach of statutory duty. The employer, therefore, might find himself being sued for substantial damages by an injured party - whether an employee or a third party - and being held liable by the court, even if both the employer and the employee honestly believed the employee to be 'self-employed'. Adequate and appropriate insurance cover is a must for all employers.

Contracts of Employment

It is important to understand that every employee *has* a contract of employment, whether it is written or not. The mere fact of offering a job to an employee, and the employee accepting that offer, brings the contract into being. The contract of employment can exist, therefore, even before the employee starts work. If there is nothing in writing, a court or tribunal, in deciding what are the terms of a contract of employment, would take account of what was agreed orally, what minimum terms are applied by law, and what terms may be 'implied' by the particular circumstances or by custom and practice in that type of business.

Main Terms

The *Employment Protection (Consolidation) Act 1978* stipulates that an employer shall provide, and an employee has the right to receive, a written statement of the *main terms* of the contract within 13 weeks of commencing work. This statement is often thought of as the contract itself; it is not. The statement is not exclusive or exhaustive, and other terms can be included or implied in the contract. It is advisable, therefore, to ensure that the whole of the contract is recorded in writing, and not just the minimum statutory 'main terms'. This is in the interests of both parties, as misunderstandings and disputes are less likely to arise.

The 'main terms' that must be included in the statement are:

- the identities of the parties (names of employer and employee);
- the date of commencement of employment;

- job title;
- whether or not any previous employment with the same or another employer is to count as part of the continuous period of this employment and, if so, the date on which continuous employment began;
- the rate of pay and the method of pay calculation;
- the intervals at which payment is to be made;
- hours of work and normal working hours (for example, 40 hours per week @ eight hours per day Monday to Friday, 8.30am to 5.30pm with one hour for lunch);
- details of holidays and holiday pay (including statutory holidays and arrangements for calculating holiday pay owed or owing when the employee leaves);
- provisions relating to incapacity and sick pay;
- pension arrangements and contributions;
- length of notice required by either side;
- details of (or reference to a further document, readily accessible, and which gives details of) disciplinary rules and procedures and grievance procedures.

Any changes to any of the terms contained in the statement must be notified to the employee in writing within one month of their taking effect.

Sample *Staff Disciplinary Procedures* are included in Appendix 4.

Implied Terms - Employees
An employee has implied duties within any contract of employment:

- to perform his duties with proper care;
- to obey the lawful and reasonable instructions of his employer;
- not to 'moonlight' in competition with his employer;
- to respect any trade secrets of his employer; and
- to respect the business confidences of his employer.

Terms in Restraint of Trade
Any term that seeks to limit a person's right to exercise his trade and earn a living is contrary to public policy and void. To be upheld, any term in a contract of employment that, for example, prohibits an employee from working for a competitor or setting up in business for himself must be

both 'reasonable' and in the interest of the parties and the public. Within these limitations, the courts will uphold an employer's right to protect trade secrets and trade connections.

What is 'reasonable' in any case depends upon the particular circumstances, but the restraint must be reasonable both geographically and in terms of time. For example, if you employ a photographer in your studio in Birmingham, it might be reasonable for the contract of employment to state that the employee is not free to set up his own competing photographic business within, say, two miles of your studio within six months of leaving your employment. To say that he can not open up a business of his own anywhere, or in the Midlands, or even anywhere in Birmingham, will almost certainly be held 'unreasonable'. So, probably, would a period of two years. The narrower the restraint is, the less likely that it will be declared void by a court. So it is better to limit the restraint to a small, definable area, only to a short time, and perhaps only to clients who were clients of your own studio during, say, the last six months of the photographer's employment with you.

Unfair Dismissal

Under the terms of the *Employment Protection (Consolidation) Act* (as amended), any employee with two years' continuous employment has the right not to be 'unfairly' dismissed; and in cases where the dismissal is on the grounds of sexual or racial discrimination (or because of trade union activity - but that does not seem to be an issue within professional photography), the two year qualifying period does not apply. And any employee who claims to have been unfairly dismissed can bring a case to an industrial tribunal, which can make orders for compensation or, more rarely, reinstatement. The amounts of compensation are often not large by High Court standards (although they can be up to £30,000 in cases of gross and blatant discrimination); but the hidden costs in management time, and perhaps in bad publicity and poor staff morale, are incalculable.

What actually constitutes unfair dismissal is difficult to define, and is usually judged individually on the merits of each case. However, the danger for employers is that an Industrial Tribunal will look not only at the merits of the case, but also at the procedures. In other words, an employer might have had very valid grounds for dismissing an employee and still be held to have dismissed unfairly if he did not go about it properly. In summary, the procedures for dismissal should include:

- the availability to all employees of a written statement of disciplinary policy, outlining both the offences liable to lead to dismissal and the procedures to be applied when dismissal is contemplated;
- the issue of prior warnings (unless the act that led to the dismissal was a case of really gross misconduct - in which case the dismissal can be without prior warnings);
- the opportunity for the employee to speak in his own defence; and
- the right of the employee to appeal against the decision to dismiss.

The list is not comprehensive and is only given here as a guide.

Discrimination

Under the respective provisions of the *Sex Discrimination Act 1975* and the *Race Relations Act 1976*, it is unlawful for an employer to discriminate on the grounds of sex or marital status or on the grounds of colour, race, nationality, or ethnic or national origin. The courts have since extended this list to include certain religious groups (notably in relation to Sikhs and the wearing of turbans). The non-discrimination provisions apply not just to the recruitment of new staff, but also to training and promotion opportunities for existing staff, and to dismissal and redundancy. It is not yet unlawful to discriminate on the grounds of age, disability or 'sexual orientation'.

There are certain very narrow exceptions to the general provisions on discrimination, and the main racial discrimination exception applicable to photography is 'where the job involves participation as an artist's or photographic model in the production of a work of art, visual image or sequence of visual images for which a person of that racial group is required for reasons of authenticity' *(Race Relations Act Section 5(2)(b))*.

Although photographic models are usually either self-employed or employed by model agencies, and not employed directly by photographers, the non discrimination provisions of the Acts extend beyond matters of employment. And within employment, the sex and race discrimination provisions actually extend to the whole of the recruitment process, with the result that an employer can actually be taken before an industrial tribunal by someone he has never employed. So an employer can avoid subsequent difficulties by making notes about job applicants and interviewees, and keeping them on file for at least six months (the time allowed for bringing a claim to an industrial tribunal). Such notes should include the genuine reason for not appointing that particular person (which should not, of course, be anything to do with the applicant's colour, racial origin, religion, sex or marital status). Without such notes, how else could an employer defend himself at an industrial tribunal, perhaps nine months after the event, against an allegation of unlawful discrimination? And an employer should never, never, ask questions at a job interview about a woman's family circumstances, or whether or not she plans to have more children, or what arrangements she makes for child care. Those questions would probably not be asked of a man or of a more mature woman, and so it amounts to discrimination to ask them of a younger woman. And nor must such factors ever be taken into account when considering promotion or redundancy either. People are entitled to be judged only on their merits and their capabilities to do the job - and that entitlement has the backing of the law.

HEALTH AND SAFETY

The law places onerous responsibilities on employers to ensure the health and safety at work of their employees. In some cases, the law also places duties on employees themselves.

There are four main acts of parliament that govern health and safety at work. They are the *Factories Act 1961*, the *Offices, Shops and Railway Premises Act 1963*, the *Fire Precautions Act 1971* and the *Health and Safety at Work Act 1974*. Additionally, there are various regulations under the acts, most notably for our purposes the *Control of Substances Hazardous to Health Regulations 1988*, known by the acronym COSHH.

The most comprehensive and wide-ranging of the four Acts referred to is the *Health and Safety at Work Act 1974*. It is intended that this Act, by way of regulations and Codes of Practice made under the Act, will eventually supersede the other three Acts entirely, so that all of the law relating to health and safety in the workplace is centred within one Act and set of regulations, and that the enforcement of all of the provisions is the responsibility of one body. Currently, however, certain aspects of the other Acts remain in force.

The Health and Safety at Work Act 1974

Application and Enforcement
The *Health and Safety at Work Act* applies to every workplace, and provides protection not just for employees but also for any person who is not an employee but who may be affected by the activities of the workplace. The only limited exception to the Act's application is that it does not apply to domestic staff.

The Act places extensive duties on both employers, employees and the self-employed. Enforcement of the Act is the responsibility of the Health and Safety Executive (HSE), whose inspectors have wide powers to enter premises, order improvements to systems by the issue of an Improvement Notice, order an immediate halt to all working by the issue of a Prohibition Notice, and to initiate criminal prosecutions for breaches of the Act or any of its regulations.

Main Duties of Employers
Every employer has a duty, so far as is reasonably practicable, to:

- provide and maintain equipment and systems of working that are safe and without risks to health;
- ensure safe arrangements for the storage, handling and transportation of articles and substances; and
- provide information, instruction, training and supervision to ensure the health and safety of his employees.

Written Safety Policy
Additional to the above general requirements, any employer having more than five employees (and employee in this context includes directors of a limited company) *must* provide a written statement of safety policy, bring the policy to the attention of all employees, and make the statement reasonably available to employees at all times. The policy has to be comprehensive, kept up to date, dated, signed by a director, partner or the proprietor, and, most importantly, the policy must actually be implemented.

First Aid Facilities and the Reporting of Accidents
Under the terms of regulations and guidance notes issued in 1981, every employer must provide first aid facilities, the very minimum (for the smallest firms or companies) being a first aid box containing six individually wrapped, sterile adhesive dressings; one large, sterile, unmedicated dressing; two triangular bandages; two safety pins; individually wrapped, moist cleaning wipes; and written first aid guidance. All accidents at work should be recorded in an Accident Book, and major accidents must be reported to the HSE.

Duties of Employees
The Act also puts a duty on every employee to take all reasonable care to ensure his own safety and that of others, and to cooperate with his employer in the implementation of safety policies and procedures.

Criminal Offences
Breach of any of the main duties imposed by the Act, and contravention of any of the regulations made under the Act, is a criminal offence. This applies equally to the duties imposed on employees. So tampering with any safety equipment (for example, recklessly or negligently emptying a fire extinguisher and failing to report it immediately so that it can be recharged) would amount to a criminal offence.

Further Information
Various publications and guidance notes, including *Writing a Health and Safety Policy Statement*, are available from the HSE. The HSE has offices in London and Sheffield, and the addresses are listed at the back of this book in Appendix 5 (page 147).

The Factories Act 1961

The Factories Act applies to any premises where people are employed in the 'making, altering, repairing, ornamenting, finishing, cleaning or washing, or adapting for sale, of any article'. If you are simply providing a photographic service and nothing further (by which is meant merely the taking of photographs and not the processing of them), then you are probably not running a factory. Even so, an industrial or commercial studio may be regarded as a factory. A photographic laboratory will almost certainly be a factory, though, as will any photographic studio with its own lab, photo-finishing or framing facilities.

The *Factories Act* provides specific duties in relation to dangerous substances and the guarding of machinery. However, it is almost certain that any duties and obligations imposed by the Act are now duplicated (and enhanced) by the *Health and Safety at Work Act* and various regulations such as COSHH.

If the *Factories Act* does apply to your premises and activities, then the local authority will have certain enforcement powers in addition to the HSE.

The Offices, Shops and Railway Premises Act 1963

If the *Factories Act* does not apply to your premises, then the *Offices, Shops and Railway Premises Act* almost certainly will! However, this Act specifically does not apply to premises where only self-employed persons work or where the only employees are close relatives of a self-employed employer. Particular provisions of the Act that still apply and that have not been 'overtaken' by the *Health and Safety at Work Act* include the duty to display extracts of the Act in poster form (we have all seen them displayed) and to notify the appropriate authority (now the HSE) when employing people for the first time at any particular premises.

The Fire Precautions Act 1971

The Fire Precautions Act provides, among other things, that any premises that are a factory, shop, railway or office must obtain a Fire Certificate if there are 20 or more people (whether employees or not) on the premises at any one time, or if there are ten or more employees who work other than on the ground floor.

The Act is enforced by, and Fire Certificates are issued by, the relevant Fire Authority.

Control of Substances Hazardous to Health

Regulations concerning the *Control of Substances Hazardous to Health* (the COSHH Regulations 1988) came fully into force at the beginning of

1990. The Regulations oblige all employers first to assess the risks associated with work involving any hazardous substance, and secondly to ensure appropriate working practices to control, minimise or eliminate such risks.

Any substance is regarded by the Regulations as being 'hazardous' if, under any other statutory requirements, it is labelled 'toxic', 'very toxic', 'harmful', 'flammable', 'corrosive', or 'irritant'. That covers just about everything: certainly it covers most photographic chemicals (and, incidentally, Tippex correction fluid, which is labelled 'harmful'). The COSHH Regulations apply to every employer in the land, and there are criminal sanctions for non-compliance.

To 'assess the risk' in accordance with the Regulations, an employer should pose himself a number of questions, and (from the point of view of evidence when an inspector calls) he should record these questions - and the answers - in writing! The questions should include: What substances are used? Where? When? How often? By whom? In what volume? How are the substances stored? . . . handled? . . . disposed of? What are the risks to employees? . . . and to any other person? What control measures are used? Are manufacturers' instructions and recommendations followed? Are all employees aware of such instructions and recommendations? What hazard does each particular substance pose? Is it corrosive? . . . toxic? . . . flammable?. What contact with the substance should be avoided? . . . inhalation? . . . eye contact? . . . skin contact? . . . swallowing?

Having asked and answered all of these questions (and the list is not exhaustive!), the employer must then act upon the answers by devising appropriate and safe working practices, make notes of all action taken, and ensure that all employees adhere to any policies laid down.

CHAPTER FIVE

PHOTOGRAPHIC COPYRIGHT

COPYRIGHT LAW IN GENERAL

A Brief Overview

What is Copyright?

Copyright is a legal and enforceable property right attaching to any 'original literary, dramatic, musical or artistic work', and is entirely distinct from the property rights in any physical material on which the work appears. The two are separate, and ownership of one does not imply ownership of the other. It is perfectly possible, and not uncommon, for the ownership of the copyright and ownership of the physical materials to be in different hands. For instance, if you buy a book, then you own the book; you do not own the copyright in any of the text or illustrations within that book. Even if you bought the original manuscript at an auction, you still own only the manuscript, not the copyright. If you commission or buy an original painting, that does not give you the right to make and sell postcards of the image, or to reproduce or exploit that painting in any way. Similarly, therefore, if a client buys a photograph from a photographer - even if it is an original transparency, and even if commissioned by that client - the client will own only the physical material, not the copyright. The photographer or other artist can, of course, sell or give away the copyright with the physical material if he chooses - or even to an unconnected third party - but unless the copyright is specifically assigned, in writing, then the copyright remains with the creator of the work.

Copyright continues in existence for 50 years after the death of the creator of the work - even if the copyright was assigned by the creator during his lifetime. If there was no lifetime assignment, copyright is dealt with on death in accordance with the normal laws of succession.

As with any other property right, copyright may be assigned to a third party. That is, it may be sold, given away, bequeathed by will, or, where there is no will, transferred under the laws of intestacy. The only stipulation on the assignment of copyright in UK law is that the assignment must be in writing signed by the copyright owner. This is one of the exceptions to the general rule of English contract law that a contract need not be in writing.

Why Copyright?
The rationale behind the concept of copyright is to protect, and thereby to encourage, the work of creative artists. If an artistic work were able to be freely exploited by anyone, without payment to its creator, then artists would cease to produce work as there would be little or no financial benefit in their doing so. Copyright protection is intended to ensure that artists retain control over any exploitation of their works, thereby ensuring a financial return to the artist for any commercial usage.

Copyright Law in the United Kingdom

The 1988 Copyright Act
The UK copyright law is contained mainly in the *Copyright, Designs and Patents Act 1988*, which came into effect on 1 August 1989. Note that it is a UK-wide Act, and so applies to Scotland and Northern Ireland as well as to England and Wales. The previous copyright Acts (of 1956 and 1911) are still relevant to some cases, as the 1988 Act is not retrospective in its application. That is to say, the 1988 Act applies only to works created or commissioned on or after 1 August 1989.

Almost all of the provisions of the Act apply automatically 'in the absence of any agreement to the contrary'. What that means is that it is possible to agree to the contrary, and override the provisions of the Act by agreement (contract).

The Act itself comprises 238 A4 pages, much of which is in detailed and technical legal language. Not all of the Act deals with copyright matters, and not all of it is relevant to photography. None the less, the reader is advised that a book such as this cannot cover such a subject more than just superficially. In complex cases, or in cases where the reader anticipates, or is likely to be involved in, litigation, further advice should be sought.

Criminal Offence
Breach of copyright is always a civil matter for which the injured party may sue in the civil courts for a variety of remedies. But most breaches

of copyright 'in the course of business', are also criminal offences, for which an offender is liable to a maximum punishment of an unlimited fine, or two years' imprisonment, or both. *(Section 107 of the Act refers.)*

PHOTOGRAPHIC COPYRIGHT IN MORE DETAIL

Copyright Protection

Definitions of 'Photograph' and 'Film'
Section 4(2) of the Act defines 'photograph' as 'a recording of light or other radiation on any medium on which an image is produced or from which an image may by any means be produced, and which is not part of a film'. (The trouble with definitions is that it often becomes necessary to define words used in definitions. Section 5(1) defines 'film' as 'recording on any medium from which a moving image may by any means be produced'. See later in this chapter under *Copyright and the Moving Image*.)

A Photograph is 'an Artistic Work'
The *Copyright, Designs and Patents Act 1988* formally recognised, for the first time, photography as an original, creative art form. As we have seen, the Act gives copyright protection to any 'original literary, dramatic, musical or artistic work' *(Section 1)*. The Act specifically includes a photograph within the definition of what is 'an artistic work', and a photograph is an artistic work 'irrespective of artistic quality' *(Section 4(1)(a))*. This is important, not merely because art is subjective, and what is artistic to one person might not be to another, but also because it eliminates any arbitrary or bureaucratic definition of what is art. Can you imagine the situation if only works 'of artistic quality' qualified for copyright protection? It would then be for a judge or civil servant inspector to determine whether any particular work was artistic enough to qualify! Thankfully, that scenario has been avoided (even though it leads to the apparent absurdity of a football league fixture list and TV listings being classed as 'literary works', and thereby protected by copyright).

Live Events Including Wedding Groups and Other Poses - not Artistic Works
Under the Act, copyright protection is given to literary, dramatic, musical and artistic works, sound recordings, films, cable and broadcast programmes and typographical arrangements, and an artistic work is

defined as being a graphic work, sculpture, collage, photograph, building, model for a building, or a work of artistic craftsmanship. It follows, therefore, that anything not appearing within that fairly comprehensive list is not afforded copyright protection. Specifically, there is no copyright in any live events, and the pose of any person(s) for a photograph, including wedding groups and bridal couples, does not amount to an artistic work and has no protection under the Act.

Many wedding photographers seem to think that they have proprietary rights over poses that they arrange. This is not so. There is nothing in copyright law to prevent any guest at a wedding photographing a wedding group that has been set and posed by another photographer, whether professional or not.

It is an infringement of copyright, however, if, without the authority of the photographer, wedding photographs (or any copyright photographs) are subsequently copied by whatever means, including by photocopying and by being recorded onto video tape.

Originality

To qualify for copyright protection, a work must be 'original' *(Section 1(1)(a))*. That is to say, there must be some skill and effort on the part of the creator. So a straight copy of another work, particularly when it is in the same medium and where there is no input of skill on the part of the copier, does not create a new copyright. A straight copy of an old, out-of-copyright photograph or of an old master, therefore, will not create a new copyright, unless the photographer uses a particular skill in the copying process. An x-ray or infra-red photograph of an old master, to examine the extent of restoration or to detect a forgery, for example, probably would create a new copyright in the photograph, as the photographer will have used skill and expertise to create a new, original work, as would a photographer using specialist lighting or filtering techniques to produce an otherwise straight photographic copy of another work. However, remember that any such copying of works that are still protected by copyright is itself a breach of copyright if done without the authority of the copyright owner.

There is no copyright in ideas; so if one photographer so likes a particular landscape photograph of another photographer, for example, and manages to recreate that photograph from the same viewpoint and in the same lighting conditions, that will not be a breach of copyright. The second photographer will have created a new, original work, itself protected by copyright. This might amount to plagiarism; but plagiarism is not a breach of copyright.

Passing Off

Continuing with the example from the immediately preceding paragraph, having created that new photograph, neither photographer can then 'pass off' the other's work as being his own. 'Passing off' is a tort (a civil wrong). In essence, passing off occurs when one person falsely represents the goods or business of another as his own, or where one person publishes a work so resembling another person's work such as to deceive the public into believing that it is that other person's work.

To succeed in an action for passing off, a plaintiff has to show that there was a misrepresentation by the defendant; that the misrepresentation was by a trader in the course of business; that it was made to a prospective customer or ultimate consumer; that it was calculated to cause, or would reasonably foreseeably cause, damage to the business or goodwill of the plaintiff; and that such damage was actually caused.

Restricted Acts, Infringements and Exceptions

By Section 16(1) of the Act, the owner of copyright in a photograph has the exclusive right to do (or to authorise the doing of) certain 'restricted acts'. These include copying the photograph, showing the photograph in public, and including the photograph in a broadcast or cable programme; and it is an infringement of copyright for any person other than the copyright owner (or person duly authorised by the copyright owner) to do any of the restricted acts. Section 17(2) defines copying as 'reproducing the work in any material form', including the storage of the work by electronic means.

The Act provides for a number of very limited exceptions to the general prohibition of 'restricted acts'. In so far as they relate to photography, these exceptions are:

1. copying for the purposes of research or private study;
2. fair dealing for the purposes of criticism or review;
3. the incidental inclusion of a protected work within another artistic work, film, broadcast or cable programme;
4. copying for the purposes of education or instruction (provided that the copy is made by the person giving or receiving instruction) or for the purposes of examinations; and
5. copying for use in parliamentary or judicial proceedings.

Photography of Buildings, Sculptures and Other Three-Dimensional Works

Although buildings, models of buildings, sculptures and other works of artistic craftsmanship enjoy copyright protection in their own right, the Act specifically permits the photographing and filming of such works without it being an infringement of copyright provided that the work is permanently situated in a public place or in premises open to the public *(Section 62)*. However, the general rule within the Act is that it is an infringement of copyright to make a two dimensional copy of a three dimensional artistic work (and, indeed, to make a three dimensional copy of a two dimensional work) *(Section 17(3))*.

Manipulation and Retouching
It is an infringement of copyright to scan a photograph into a computer without the authority of the copyright owner *(Section 17(2))*. Further, any subsequent electronic manipulation, or, indeed, any manual retouching of a photograph without the consent of the copyright owner, is an infringement of the moral right relating to the derogatory treatment of a work (see later under *Moral Rights*).

When any such manipulation or retouching (whether manual or electronic) is done with the authority of the copyright owner, the subsequent altered image will be the subject of a new copyright in its own right, jointly owned by the owner of the copyright in the original image and the retoucher. At some point, if the original image is manipulated to such a degree as to bear no resemblance to the original image, the resultant copyright will probably belong solely to the manipulator, while the original copyright owner retains copyright in the original image.

To Claim Copyright Protection
No formal procedures are necessary to claim copyright in a photograph. Copyright in a photograph exists from the moment of creation of the latent image. There are no requirements to register the copyright with any government body or agency, and there are no legal requirements even to publicise the existence or ownership of copyright on the photograph. However, that is not true in all countries in the world, and so the practice of proclaiming copyright has grown up. This is usually done by use of the internationally-recognised copyright symbol of a letter 'c' enclosed within a circle (thus: ©) followed by the author's name and the year of creation. Hence you will see the imprint '© *Adrian Berkeley 1993'* at the start of this book.

Although there is no requirement for such an imprint in order for copyright to exist or to be effective, use of such an imprint nevertheless alerts anyone and everyone to the fact that the copyright exists, and so nobody can claim ignorance of the fact.

It is strongly recommended, therefore, that all photographs bear such an imprint, on the backs of prints and on transparency mounts. A small amount of additional wording might also useful, such as, for example: *'© XYZ Studios Ltd 1993. Tel 071 123 1234. Any unauthorised reproduction is unlawful and may be a criminal offence'.*

Ownership of Copyright

The 1988 Act - The General Rule
The Act goes on to provide that the first owner of copyright in an artistic work is its 'author' *(Section 11(1))* and that the author of a work is the person who creates it *(Section 9(1))*. In the case of a photograph, this means the photographer. The term 'first owner' is important. It is a recognition of the fact that, as we have seen, copyright can subsequently be assigned by the owner. But it does mean that unless and until the photographer actually takes the positive step of assigning his copyright (in writing, and signed), the photographer remains the owner.

The 1988 Act totally reversed the previous position on ownership of copyright in a photograph. The position now is that the first owner of the copyright is the photographer, whether the photograph was commissioned or not. Previously, the copyright was owned by the commissioning client in the case of a commissioned photograph, and, in the case of a non-commissioned photograph, by the owner of the film at the time the photograph was taken. Remember, though, that the previous rule still applies to photographs taken before 1 August 1989.

Employed Photographers
The Act makes one very important exception to the general rule that the first owner of the copyright in a photograph is the photographer, and this relates to photographers who are employees. In the case of a photograph taken by an employee 'in the course of his employment', the first owner of the copyright is the employer *(Section 11(2))*. The Act defines 'employee' as one who is engaged under 'a contract of service' (as opposed to a contract *for services*) *(Section 178)*. The distinction between a contract of service and a contract for services is crucial, and is explained in some detail on pages 49 and 50 in the previous chapter (EMPLOYMENT LAW).

The phrase 'in the course of his employment' in the above paragraph is important. Clearly an employed photographer is fully entitled to take private photographs in his own time, using his own equipment and his own materials; indeed he may even borrow equipment from his employer. He is also entitled, provided it does not breach any express or implied term of his contract of employment, to 'moonlight' as a freelance. In such cases, the employed photographer would not be acting 'in the course of his employment', and would therefore be the first owner of the copyright in any photographs he takes under those circumstances.

Another important point to note is that the provision in the Act whereby the copyright is owned by the employer can be overridden by agreement. That is to say, the contract of employment between the employer and the employed photographer may contain a term giving ownership of the copyright in any photographs taken 'in the course of employment' to the employee. Such a term would be valid, and would override the contrary provision of the Act.

In the light of the provisions relating to copyright ownership, and the importance of the distinction between an employee and one who is self-employed, the practice of some photographers of 'employing' part-time operators to assist with workload fluctuations (perhaps Saturdays only during the wedding season, for example) needs careful handling and consideration. If the part-time operator is genuinely an employee and is engaged under a 'contract of service' *(see Chapter 4)*, then the copyright in any photographs taken by the employee in the course of that employ-ment is owned by the employer. However, if the part-time operator is, in reality, self-employed, engaged under a 'contract for services', then it is the part-time operator himself who will own the copyright (which may not be what was intended!). Any 'employer' who finds himself in the position of engaging a self-employed operator can cover himself so far as the copyright aspects are concerned by insisting on the operator signing a declaration to the effect that copyright in all photography undertaken for and on behalf of the 'employer' and while engaged by the employer is assigned to and vested in the employer.

Students and Colleges
The provision of the Act relating to the ownership of copyright in works created by photographers engaged under a 'contract of service' applies equally to those engaged under a 'contract of apprenticeship'. However, as a student at a college or university is engaged neither under a contract of service nor a contract of apprenticeship, the logic of the Act is that a photography student owns the copyright in any work he produces as part of his course, even if any materials are supplied by and owned by the college. This may not present a problem to the college or the tutors; indeed the course tutors may think it only right and proper that students should own the copyright in their works. But if it does present a problem, then the college authorities should obtain a blanket assignment of copy-right from each student as a condition of the offer of a place on the course, or at least a blanket licence allowing the college to reproduce,

exhibit and display (but not for commercial exploitation) any photographs taken by the student as part of the course. Such an assignment must be in writing, (and any licence really ought to be in writing) signed by the student, and should to refer to all photographs made in the course of instruction.

Ownership Under the 1956 Act

Bear in mind that the 1988 Act only operates in relation to photographs taken on or after 1 August 1989. Photographs taken before that date come under the terms of the 1956 Act (or, for even older photographs, the 1911 Act).

Copyright in a photograph to which the 1956 Act applies belongs to the commissioning client in the case of commissioned photography, and in the case of non-commissioned photography, to the person who owned the film (or other material) at the time the photograph was taken.

The position of some employed photographers was also slightly different under the 1956 Act. If the photographer was employed by a newspaper, periodical or magazine, then the employer owns all rights in relation to publication of the photograph in newspapers, periodicals and magazines, but the photographer owns all remaining publication rights. The position of all other employees under the 1956 Act is the same as for the 1988 Act.

Duration of Copyright

Duration Under the 1988 Act

Copyright in a photograph to which the 1988 Act applies lasts for 50 years from the end of the year in which the photographer dies *(Section 12(1))*. This remains true even if the photographer parts with the copyright at any time during his lifetime, and even if it is assigned immediately the photograph is created. The duration of the copyright protection has nothing to do with who owns the copyright; it is related only to the creator.

In the case of copyright in a photograph created by an employee in the course of his employment, the Act still seems to regard the employed photographer as the author or creator of the photograph *(Section 9(1))*, even though it is the employer who owns the copyright *(Section 11(2))*. So the copyright would seem to last until 50 years after the death of the employee! Whether that is what parliament intended when it enacted the Act, and whether that is the interpretation that a court might apply, are difficult to assess; but that is certainly the literal interpretation.

Duration Under the 1956 and 1911 Acts

Copyright in a photograph to which the 1956 Act applies (that is, any photograph taken on or after 1 June 1957) expires 50 years from the end of the year in which the photograph was first published. If the photograph has never been published, then copyright expires on 31 December 2039.

Copyright in a photograph taken prior to 1 June 1957, to which the 1911 Act applies, expires 50 years from the end of the year in which the photograph was taken.

Copyright: Assignment and Licences

The owner of the copyright in a photograph has certain exclusive rights in relation to the copying or showing of that photograph in public, or to authorise such copying or showing (see above under *Restricted Acts, Infringements and Exceptions*). The granting of such authority is more properly referred to as the granting of a 'licence'.

Assignment of Copyright

By Section 90 of the Act, copyright may be assigned in writing signed by or on behalf of the copyright owner, or it may be assigned by will or, where there is no will, by the operation of the laws of intestacy. When a copyright is assigned or inherited, any rights already granted by way of licence are still valid, and are binding on any person to whom the copyright is transferred.

Do I Need to Assign my Copyright?

Usually, the answer to this is 'no'. Most requirements of clients can be met adequately by the granting of suitable and appropriate licences. A client who insists on assignment of the copyright probably has no understanding of copyright law and licences, and is merely seeking to protect his interests in the way that *he* thinks is appropriate. There may be certain, very limited instances where assignment of copyright might be appropriate, for example if you are undertaking commissions of particular sensitivity. This might be anything from a commercial commission from a government defence contractor to a commission for private boudoir photography. In cases where a client insists on assignment of copyright, he may well also insist on acquiring ownership of all negatives.

Copyright is not sacrosanct! If a client absolutely insists on assignment of copyright as a condition of the commission, then you will probably have to go along with it. But clients must understand that a professional photographer earns his living by the creation and exploitation of photographic images, and that if they want assignment of the copyright, there will be a commercial price to pay for it! But the general rule for any photographer must be to resist very strongly any pressures to part with copyright.

Licences

Unlike the assignment of copyright (which must be in writing, signed by the copyright owner), a licence need not be in writing to be lawful and effective, unless it is an 'exclusive licence'. An exclusive licence is 'a licence in writing signed by or on behalf of the copyright owner authorising the licensee to the exclusion of all other persons, including the person granting the licence, to exercise a right which would otherwise be exercisable exclusively by the copyright owner'. A licence that is not exclusive may be granted orally. However, it is strongly recommended that all licences are at least noted in writing, and preferably acknowledged in writing by the licensee (the person to whom the licence is granted). It should go without saying that in terms of evidence in the event of a dispute, oral agreements are far less satisfactory than written agreements (or, at the very least, agreements that are some way evidenced in writing).

Terms of Licences

A copyright owner is free to grant licences on whatever terms he wishes and which he can agree with the prospective licensee. Generally, a licence will need to cover three particular considerations:

1. the geographical extent of the licence;
2. the time extent of the licence; and
3. the nature of the rights that the licence seeks to grant.

The geographical extent of the licence, for example, may be worldwide, UK only, European Community only, USA only, UK and north America, EC and USA, the Commonwealth countries, or perhaps just Scotland only. These are only examples; the geographical extent of the licence may be as restrictive or extensive as the copyright owner and the licensee agree, provided that it is clear and identifiable.

So, too, with the time extent of the licence (except, of course, that it can not extend beyond the duration of the copyright). The licence may be for one year, three years, five years, or any fixed term, or expressed as until the 31 December 2035. Indeed it can be expressed to be for any time up to 50 years less one day after the end of the year in which the photographer dies, or it may be expressed to be for the duration of the existence of the copyright. The copyright owner and the licensee are free to agree to whatever length term they wish, and to express it how they wish.

The nature of the rights granted may be for publication in newspapers, or newspapers and periodicals, or for book covers up to a maximum of, say, 10,000 copies. The licence may also be expressed to be exclusive (for the duration and within the geographical limits agreed) or non-exclusive. If an exclusive licence is granted, the copyright owner cannot subsequently grant another licence to another party which conflicts with the exclusive rights of the first licensee. If the licence is not exclusive, the copyright owner is free to grant other licences to other users. Once again, the copyright owner and the licensee are free to agree whatever terms they wish; and the payment will vary accordingly.

Implied Licences

When photography is commissioned, and there is no formal agreement (whether written or oral) as to the terms of the licence granted to the commissioning client, there will be an implied term that the client may use the photography for the purposes and to the extent for which it was commissioned. Any further use would really require the granting of a further licence. However, in such circumstances, any dispute would ultimately be a case of one person's word or understanding against another's. Disputes and misunderstandings are best avoided by the use of clear, written agreements.

Copyright and Licence: Freehold and Leasehold

To assist in understanding the relationship between copyright and licence(s), and between the copyright owner and licensee(s), it is useful to consider the analogy of freehold land, leasehold land, and rights of way. The owner of freehold land owns the land absolutely and outright. He can grant leases of all or part of his land, and he can grant rights of way over his land. Having been granted a lease or a right of way, the holder of the lease or the right of way acquires certain legal rights, in return for which the freeholder accepts certain restrictions and obligations. The freeholder cannot take away those rights, and nor can he grant any further rights to any other party that conflict with or limit the rights already granted.

In copyright terms, the copyright owner is the freeholder, and the licensee is the person who buys the lease or the right of way. And so once a licence under the copyright has been granted, on whatever terms, the licensee acquires legal rights, and the copyright owner cannot revoke the licence (other than on conditions contemplated and provided for within the licence agreement) and he cannot grant any further licences that conflict with or impinge upon the rights of the first licensee.

Moral Rights

The 1988 Act introduced, for the first time in UK law, the concept of 'moral rights'. Given that they are now enshrined within the Act, they are actually legal, statutory rights; nevertheless, the Act itself uses the term 'moral rights'.

In summary, these rights are threefold:

1. the right of the author of a work to be identified as such (known colloquially as the 'right of paternity');
2. the right of the author to object to derogatory treatment of the work (known as the 'right of integrity'); and
3. the right of any person not to have work falsely attributed to him.

Additionally, there are circumstances in which a client has a right to privacy of certain photographs and films.

The Right to be Identified as Author

This right is granted by Section 77 of the Act, and applies to the author of a photograph and to the director of a film.

The author of a photograph has the right to be identified as such whenever the photograph is published commercially or exhibited in public (including as part of a film, broadcast or cable programme). The identification must be 'clear and reasonably prominent'.

For this right to be effective, it must first be asserted in writing, signed by the photographer (or director) *(Section 78)*. Assertion of this right may be for a specific work, or for a specific work for a specific client or use, or it may be general. Wording of such an assertion should be to the effect of *'The moral rights conferred by the Copyright, Designs and Patents Act 1988 are hereby asserted'*.

However, having granted the right, Section 79 of the Act then specifies a wide range of exceptions where the right does not apply, including:

- if the image was computer-generated;
- if the first owner of the copyright was the photographer's employer;
- if the photograph was made for the purpose of reporting current events; and
- when the photograph is published in a newspaper, magazine, other

periodical, encyclopaedia, dictionary, yearbook or other collective reference work.

Notwithstanding the wide exceptions listed above, it is the practice of most newspaper, magazine and book publishers to give credits to photographers when asked; but the photographer has no right to insist (other than by refusing permission for the photograph to be published).

The Right to Object to Derogatory Treatment
Under Section 80, a photographer has the right to object to any derogatory treatment of his photograph. This means by way of manipulation of the image, cropping, reverse printing, inclusion of the photograph in a montage or compilation, and so forth. But the treatment must actually be 'derogatory' (that is, it must be capable of damaging the photographer's reputation).This right exists without having to be positively asserted, but is subject to similar wide-ranging exceptions as for the Right to be Identified as Author under Section 77 (above).

The Right Against False Attribution
So far as photography is concerned, this is the right not to be falsely credited as the creator of a photograph (but, as with the other moral rights, it applies also to any artistic, literary, dramatic or musical work). This right, granted by Section 84, applies to any person, and the right does not need to be asserted.

The rationale behind this right is that the reputation of an artist may be damaged by a false attribution, particularly, of course, where the work in question is of a low standard or is in some other way detrimental. There may be cases, of course, where false attribution of work so damages an artist's reputation that an action for libel might be appropriate.

A Client's Right to Privacy
Given that a commissioning client now no longer owns the copyright in any photography he commissions, the Act *(Section 85)* gives limited rights of privacy to any person who commissions a photograph (or film) 'for private and domestic purposes'. Clearly this will include most wedding and portrait photography.

In summary, any such a photograph (or film) may not be issued to the public, exhibited or shown in public, or included in a broadcast or cable programme without the consent of the client. The client does not have to assert this right; rather, the reverse operates, in that the right exists unless and until the client agrees otherwise. And a client's agreement may subsequently be withdrawn.

The Act is ambiguous as to whether the client's consent needs to be in writing. So until there is a binding judicial interpretation of the consent requirements, it is advisable to ensure that such consents are obtained in writing, signed by the client.

Wedding and portrait photographers should therefore ensure that such a condition is included within their *Terms and Conditions of Business*. However, given the possible requirement of the Act for such consents to be in writing and signed, it should become normal practice for social photographers to obtain a signature of acceptance of the *Terms of Business* from every client.

And if you think that you are unlikely ever to want to exhibit or show the photograph in public, remember that any submission of a photograph to any competition, whether for marketing or professional purposes, or to any qualifications panel of the various professional bodies, or any exhibition of a photograph in a studio display, amounts to 'exhibiting in public' for these purposes.

The Effect of Death and Assignment on Moral Rights

Moral rights are not capable of assignment, other than by bequest or by operation of the rules of intestacy. In the event of copyright being assigned by the photographer during his lifetime, the moral rights stay with the photographer. After the death of the photographer, the moral rights transfer to his heirs, and, in the case of the right of paternity and right of integrity, continue in existence for the entire duration of the copyright. The right to object to false attribution lasts for 20 years after a person's death.

Remedies for Infringement

Infringement of any of the rights conferred by the Act - whether infringement of the copyright itself, infringement of a moral right, or infringement of the rights of a licensee under the copyright - are actionable in the civil courts by the owner of that right. The remedies available to an offended party are detailed in Sections 96-103 of the Act.

Criminal Penalties

Remember, too, that there are many and wide-ranging criminal offences under the Act. Basically, any person who, without the authority of the copyright owner, does any of the following in relation to an infringing copy, commits a criminal offence:

- makes for sale or hire;
- in the course of business, sells or lets for hire, offers or exposes for sale or hire, exhibits in public or distributes;
- possesses in the course of business with a view to committing an infringing act;
- imports into the UK other than for private and domestic use; or
- distributes, otherwise than in the course of business, to such an extent as to prejudice the owner of the copyright.

These offences apply also to copies that infringe the rights of an exclusive licensee under the copyright. So having granted an exclusive licence to a client, the photographer himself would be committing a criminal offence if he did any of the above things in contravention of the rights of the licensee, even though the photographer might still be the owner of the copyright!

The maximum penalties on conviction of most of these offences are an unlimited fine, or two years' imprisonment, or both.

Civil Remedies

INJUNCTION: If you become aware before the event of any plans to infringe your copyright, you may apply to the court for an injunction to prevent any such infringement. After the event, you may seek an injunction to prevent any further infringement. Any party in breach of an injunction will be in contempt of court (a criminal offence, and one with which the courts have wide powers to deal).

DAMAGES: Your normal remedy after the event will be monetary damages (perhaps combined with an injunction). Damages will normally be the amount that the offending party would have paid for a licence if a licence had in fact been granted. But by Section 97(2), 'The court may, having regard to all the circumstances, and in particular to the flagrancy of the infringement and any benefit accruing to the defendant, award such additional damages as the justice of the case may require'.

Damages can be significant, as the case of *Williams v Settle [1960]* demonstrates. In that case, a photographer sold wedding pictures to a newspaper (because someone featured in the pictures had become a murder victim). The wedding clients owned the copyright and sued the photographer for damages. They were awarded £1,000 (a very substantial sum in 1960), and the award was upheld by the Court of Appeal. In its judgement, the Court of Appeal referred to the flagrancy of the case and to the total disregard of the photographer, not just of the legal rights of the defendants but of their feelings too.

ACCOUNT OF PROFITS: On the principle that a plaintiff cannot be paid twice for one infringement of copyright, this remedy is available as an alternative to damages, not additional to damages. An Account of Profit requires the defendant to pay the plaintiff all net profits arising out of the infringement.

DELIVERY UP: The court may also order the 'delivery up' to the plaintiff of all infringing copies of the work. The reasoning behind this remedy is that any infringing copies of a copyright work belong to the copyright owner. It was on this basis that a government minister was able to claim ownership of photocopies of government documents that had been leaked to *The Guardian* newspaper by a civil servant *(Secretary of State for Defence v Guardian Newspapers Ltd [1985])* and obtain 'delivery up' of the copies of the documents.

REMEDY FOR INFRINGEMENT OF MORAL RIGHTS: The remedy in the case of infringement of moral rights may be either damages for breach of contract (if the assertion of the infringed moral right was part of the contract with a client) or, where there is no contract, for damages for the tort (civil wrong) of breach of statutory duty *(Section 103(1)).*

Ignorance is a Defence!
Your client may well have a defence under Section 97(1) of the Act which (extraordinarily in English law) allows ignorance as a defence! Section 97(1) in full states that:

> Where in an action for infringement of copyright it is shown that at the time of the infringement the defendant did not know, and had no reason to believe, that copyright subsisted in the work to which the action relates, the plaintiff is not entitled to damages against him, but without prejudice to any other remedy.

Whereas a Section 97 defence might be available to an inexperienced buyer of photography, it is highly unlikely that an experienced buyer of photography, or anyone whose business is in photography, reprography, printing, publishing, advertising or public relations, (and there are no doubt others) would be able to rely on Section 97.

Whom to Sue

A single infringement of copyright may amount to a wrongdoing by more than one person. For instance, if a photograph taken by you and in which you still own the copyright is taken by your client, without your authority, to another photographer, a photographic laboratory or to a high street copy shop for copying (whether by way of an inter-neg or just photocopying), and a copy is in fact made, both your client and the trader supplying the copy have infringed your copyright. You can sue either of them individually, or you can sue them both jointly (but you cannot sue them both individually and obtain damages twice over).

In deciding which offending party to sue, bear in mind the likely resources of each prospective defendant, for it is no use suing someone on a low income or with few or no assets, and bear in mind the Section 97 defence outlined above.

A portrait photographer in Yorkshire learned that a photograph in which he owned the copyright had been taken by his client to a photographic laboratory for copying, and had in fact been copied. Against the advice of his professional association, the photographer sued his client and not the laboratory. Even though the photographer's copyright notice was on the back of the photograph, the client successfully relied on Section 97 and the photographer lost the case. (He later sued the laboratory and won, even though the laboratory tried to rely on an indemnity which it had obtained from the client. The indemnity did not allow the laboratory to turn a blind eye to what it knew, or ought to have known, to be the true situation.)

Copyright and the Moving Image

General

The definition of 'film' given in the Act is 'A recording on any medium from which a moving image may by any means be produced'. A 'film' therefore means any moving image, and includes cinematographic or video-tape productions, video discs, computer-generated animations, and rapid, multi-projector slide programmes.

A film is not within the Act's definition of 'artistic work', but a film is nevertheless protected by copyright *(Section 1(1)(b))*.

The 'author' in relation to a film is 'the person by whom the arrangements necessary for the making of the film are undertaken' *(Section 9(2)(a))*. By complex cross-referencing between other Sections of the Act, it can be ascertained that the author is not necessarily the director, but the producer or the director's employer. However, it is the director (even though he is not 'the author') who has the moral rights under Section 77 to be identified whenever the film is shown or broadcast and under Section 80 not to have the film subjected to derogatory treatment.

Unlike the case of still photography, copyright in a film expires 50 years from the end of the year in which it is released, or, if it is not released, 50 years from the end of the year in which it was made *(Section 13)*.

Rights of Other Artists

The question of copyright in moving image productions is infinitely more complex than copyright in stills photography, mainly because of the numerous complementary, parallel and subsidiary rights of other creative and performing artists. Beyond what has already been said, copyright in moving image productions is outside the scope of this book. Suffice to say that just about everyone involved in a moving image production acquires rights - either copyright or rights in performance: there are the producer and the director (as we have seen), and there are the script-writer, the music composer, the music arranger, the orchestra and other music performers, the actors, the set-designers, the costume designers and, of course, the cinematographer. There are others too! And to complicate matters still further, many of these are often joint rights holders (for example where two writers collaborate on the script).

Ownership of Negatives and Other Materials

Strictly speaking, ownership of negatives and other photographic materials is not a matter of copyright. It has already been noted elsewhere in the chapter that ownership of copyright and ownership of the physical materials are two entirely different things. However, it seems appropriate to comment briefly here on the ownership of photographic materials, as many photographers and clients still seem to confuse the ownership of materials and the ownership of the copyright.

Negatives

There is no specific statutory guidance on the ownership of negatives (or of original transparencies for that matter), and so we are left with applying the general law. It would seem to be the case that, in the absence of any agreement to the contrary, photographic negatives remain the property of whoever owned the film at the time the photograph was taken. This will usually be the photographer. However, there is a duty on the photographer to retain negatives in good condition and for a reasonable period, to allow a client to order subsequent reprints. That 'reasonable period' has been held by a court (but not such as to create a binding precedent) to be ten years.

An 'agreement to the contrary' would include any case where the photographer has either quoted or invoiced for 'film' or 'materials'. The logic of this is obvious: if you invoice a client for any physical thing, and the client pays that invoice, then the client owns the thing that he has paid for. So if you want to retain ownership of your negatives (and most photographers do), then never use the word 'film' or the word 'materials' in any quotations or invoices. You can quote and invoice on a daily rate, on an hourly rate, or even on a 'per shot' rate and include the cost of any materials as just another overhead (without mentioning them) within your quoted rate. That way, you will retain ownership of your negatives.

Transparencies

In the case of original transparencies made as part of a commission by a client for original photography, those transparencies actually passed to the client will, in the absence of any agreement to the contrary, become the property of the client. Any transparencies not passed to the client (for example, bracketing shots, or duplicate shots for the photographer's library use) will remain the property of the photographer.

You can get around the problem of the client owning your original transparencies (if indeed it is a problem) by not quoting or invoicing for 'film' or 'materials' (see above under *Negatives*) and making it plain to the client before or at the time of the commission that the transparencies are handed over only on permanent loan, or on loan for the duration of the copyright licence that you are granting. This would amount to an 'agreement to the contrary'.

Original transparencies handed to a client on loan, as from the photographer's library or agency, for example, will, of course, remain the property of the photographer.

Prints

Any prints passed to a client will become the property of the client, and there is no particular need to agree anything to the contrary.

Crown Copyright

By Section 163 of the Act, any work made either by Her Majesty or by an officer or servant of the Crown in the course of his duties is subject to Crown Copyright, which means that Her Majesty is the first owner of the copyright and that copyright lasts for 125 years. The main point of relevance here, though, is that if a photographer who is *not* an officer or servant of the Crown (and a servant in this context is someone who is employed under a contract of service - for which see Chapter 4 - EMPLOYMENT LAW) is commissioned by a government department to take photographs, then it is the photographer (or his employer, as the case may be) who owns the copyright, not Her Majesty. This is contrary to the belief of some photographers - and indeed of some officers of government departments - that work carried out for the Crown automatically comes under the Crown Copyright provisions.

International Aspects of Copyright Law

This area of the law is very complex, not only in its direct substance, but also in terms of its application. Basically, the UK is a signatory (along with most other countries in the world) to both the Berne Convention of 1886 (as subsequently amended) and the Universal Copyright Convention of 1952. Under the terms of these Conventions, a signatory country agrees to afford the same degree of copyright protection to citizens of other signatory countries as it does to its own citizens, and to respect and uphold the copyright laws of other signatory countries. This is a gross over-simplification, of course, and the costs involved in trying to enforce your rights will probably be, so far as photography is concerned anyway, out of proportion to any damage suffered.

European Considerations

As part of the move to a single market, the European Commission (of the EC) is currently engaged in the harmonisation of copyright laws throughout the Community. The intention is that this will be done piecemeal, one aspect at a time, and it will be many years before the UK copyright laws outlined in this chapter are replaced totally by EC-wide copyright laws.

The first aspect to which the Commission is giving attention is the duration of copyright. The intention throughout will be to harmonise upwards rather than to reduce everything to the lowest common denominator, and the proposal so far as duration is concerned is to raise it to the current highest level within any Community country, 70 years after the death of the creator (as opposed to the 50 years current in the UK). Unless and until any EC-wide provisions are agreed (which they have not been at the time of writing), the UK law as contained in the *Copyright, Designs and Patents Act 1988* will remain applicable.

CHAPTER SIX

TORTS (CIVIL WRONGS)

GENERAL

What is a 'Tort'?

Put very simply, a tort is a civil wrong (as opposed to a criminal wrong) which is neither a breach of contract nor a breach of trust, and which gives rise to legal rights and remedies for the person wronged and legal liability on the part of the wrongdoer. (We have already dealt with contract law in previous chapters; the law of trusts is another specialist division of the law, administered by the Chancery Division of the High Court, and which need not concern us in this book.)

Principal torts include:

- Negligence
- Nuisance
- Trespass
- Conversion
- Breach of Statutory Duty, and
- Defamation (libel and slander)

We shall look briefly at each of these torts in turn a little later, but first we shall look at some of the generalities relating to torts.

Damage and Liability

Generally, the person wronged has to prove that he has suffered actual damage as a result of the tort. The two exceptions to this are in actions for trespass and actions for libel (but not slander). In trespass and libel cases, it is only necessary to prove that the trespass or the libel has occurred, irrespective of whether damage was suffered as a result.

Conversely, not all actions that cause damage amount to torts. If another photographer opens a business next door to your business, as a result of which your business suffers damage, no tort has been committed.

Liability

The general rule is that all persons and corporate bodies are liable for their actions in tort. There are certain exceptions to the general rule, including cases where the alleged wrongdoer is an infant or a minor and where the tort is based on malice or negligence (where age will be a relevant factor in determining whether the infant or minor is in fact liable), and cases in which trades unions enjoy immunity for certain acts done in the course or furtherance of a trade dispute.

To be held liable for any damage suffered (where it is necessary actually to prove damage), the damage must either be a direct consequence of the wrongful act or be such that a reasonable person would have foreseen the possibility of that damage resulting from the wrongful act. (The test of 'reasonable foreseeability' is therefore very similar to that in cases of breach of contract, discussed earlier in this book.)

Liability for the Torts of Others

This is known as 'vicarious liability', and there are two instances of vicarious liability that might be of concern to us.

First, parents are not automatically liable for the torts of their children; as we have just seen above, children are generally liable for their own torts. But a parent can be vicariously liable for the torts of children where the parent has authorised, ordered or condoned the commission of a tort. Secondly, and of particular importance to those in business, an employer is vicariously liable for the torts of his employees committed in the course of employment.

The liability of an employer for the torts of his employees is an onerous one, and largely revolves around the old thorny question of whether the 'employee' is engaged under a contract of service (in which case he is an employee) or a contract for services (in which case he is a self-employed, independent contractor). (For details of the distinction between a contract of service and a contract for services, see Chapter 4, EMPLOYMENT LAW.) In essence, though, an employer will be liable for the torts of his employees where the tort (whether by act or omission) was expressly or implicitly authorised by the employer; where the tort arose out of an unauthorised manner of doing an authorised act; and where the employer retrospectively condones or authorises it.

The liability of an employer does not affect the parallel liability of the employee. The employee still remains personally liable, and the injured party can sue either or both.

The employer will not be liable, however, in cases where the employee (to use the quaint, legal phraseology) 'goes off on a frolic of his own'. So, for example, if you send your delivery driver to deliver some transparencies to a client, and, on the way, your driver makes a detour to have a cup of tea with his mum and, while on his detour, throws a lighted cigarette out of the van window setting fire to a baby's pram, you will not be liable (unless, by turning a blind eye to this type of behaviour in the past, you have condoned or 'authorised' his unofficial detours).

In the case of torts committed by independent contractors (those engaged under a contract *for services*), the general rule is that the 'employer' is not liable. As with most areas of law, though, there are the black and white areas and there are the grey areas. If you call in a plumber to do some work in your darkroom, and by his negligent use of his blow torch he sets fire to your lab manager's overcoat hanging up nearby, then it is the plumber who is liable, not you. But you may be liable if you engage an independent contractor to do something that itself constitutes a tort (nuisance or trespass, for example) or that is inherently an extra hazardous activity in itself. (Incidentally, the legal authority for the latter proposition actually concerned a photographer. The owners of a cinema engaged contractors to carry out some work on the cinema, and the contractors in turn engaged photographers to take some flash photographs. It was 1934, and flash photography was then an 'extra hazardous activity' entailing the use of magnesium powder. The flash powder ignited and set fire to the cinema. The original contractors were held liable to the cinema owners, but the original contractors could claim, in turn, against the photographers. *(Honeywill & Stein v Larkin Brothers [1934])*

Remoteness of Damage

In addition to being liable for any direct damage suffered as a result of his tort, a wrongdoer will also be liable for other damage that follows naturally from the wrongful act and which a reasonable person would have foreseen. There has to come a point, though, at which the wrongdoer ceases to be held liable for consequences that follow from his wrongful act. When this point is reached (and it will be different in every case, dependent upon the particular circumstances), the damage is said to be too remote from the original act, and so the wrongdoer will not be held liable.

By way of example, if you are out on a photographic assignment and you drop a tripod from a scaffold on to someone's head, you will be liable (in the tort of negligence) for damage to that person. You will also be liable for any loss of earnings on the part of that person as a result of his having to take time off work. You will probably also be liable if he has to cancel an imminent family holiday as a result of your negligence. Those things are reasonably foreseeable as the consequences of your negligence. But if his wife is involved in a road accident whilst on her way to visit him in hospital you will not be liable, even though it could be said with some justification that she would not have been travelling on that road at that time, and would not have had the accident, but for your original negligence in dropping a tripod on her husband's head, causing him to be hospitalised.

Remember, too, that you would be equally liable if, in the above example, the photographer who dropped the tripod was not you, but your employee acting in the course of his employment.

General Defences to Actions in Tort

We shall look later at some of the defences available in specific torts (notably libel), but the following are general defences that are available in an action for tort:

Consent

This defence is generally given a Latin name; but Latin has been rigorously avoided throughout this book, and so we shall just refer to it as 'consent'. It applies on the basis that 'no injury can be done to a willing party'. A Rugby player, for example, consents to the risk of some degree of injury, and anyone injuring him within the course of a game and within the laws of the game would have a legitimate defence. 'Within the laws of the game' is important; the rugby player does not necessarily consent to injuries inflicted outside of the laws of the game. The same principle will apply to sports photographers, for example. A photographer perched right on the goal-line at a football match is running the risk of being hit by the ball or by a player; but he must be said to have consented to such a risk. That does not mean that he consents to a player deliberately kicking the ball directly at him. Furthermore, mere knowledge of a risk does not amount to consent; there must be actual consent, and the consent has to be genuine. It may be express (positive written or oral consent) or it may be implied from behaviour or circumstances. To use the example of the rugby player again, he is implying his consent to the risk by taking part in the game; and the sports photographer is consenting to the risk by placing himself near to the action.

Necessity

Necessity is available as a defence, though it is rare. The alleged wrong-doer would need to show that he committed the tort in question in order to prevent a greater evil. An obvious and simple example would be a trespass on someone's private property to rescue someone from a fire on that property or on a neighbouring property.

Self Defence

Any person may use proportionate and reasonable force to defend himself or others, and to a lesser degree his property or that of others. This is usually a defence against an action for trespass (whether to the person, to land or to goods) but it is possible to imagine circumstances where it might be used as a defence in a negligence case. But note that the force used must be both reasonable and proportionate, and note also that you *may* not have a defence where physical force is used to defend property rather than people. You certainly cannot shoot someone who trespasses on your land, or even who uses or threatens unarmed physical violence (unless that use or threat of physical violence is so extreme as to make shooting the perpetrator both 'reasonable' and 'proportionate' in the circumstances). Obviously it is not possible to detail every circumstance where the defence may be available in an action for tort, or to predict the findings of the courts. 'Reasonable' and 'proportionate' are the watch-words, and if the situation should arise, try to err on the side of caution.

Statutory Authority

It is a defence in an action for tort to show that there was a statutory authority for the alleged wrongdoer to carry out the act complained of. The public utility companies, for example, may create a nuisance by digging up the road near your premises, but they have the statutory authority to do so. Likewise, a police officer or a Health and Safety Inspector, for example, has powers of entry into premises in certain circumstances; so what might otherwise be a trespass is rendered not so by the defence of statutory authority. However, to continue with the latter example, the defence would not be available to anyone with the statutory authority to enter your premises who exceeded or abused that authority; and his presence on your property would become a trespass (not merely from the time of the excess or abuse of authority, but from the very beginning).

Justification

Justification is available as a defence to libel and to trespass to land. In so far as it relates to libel, the defence will be discussed more fully later in this chapter. So far as trespass to land is concerned, the defence is similar to the defence of 'statutory authority', but may extend, for example, to bailiffs lawfully entering premises to eject a tenant, and to entry onto another's land in cases of emergency (in which case it is very similar to the defence of 'necessity').

Mistake is no Defence

A mistake of law is no defence to an action in tort. That is, it is no use merely saying that you were not aware that your action (or omission, as the case may be) was unlawful and amounted to a tort. The general principle that 'ignorance of the law is no excuse' applies.

The same applies as to a mistake of fact (that is, it is no defence to an action in tort), though there are certain very narrow and very limited exceptions, which need not concern us.

Remedies

The usual remedies available are damages by way of monetary compensation and injunctions to restrain the wrongdoer from committing similar torts in the future.

Some specific torts have other specific remedies available. These will be referred to individually under discussion of the relevant torts (below)

SPECIFIC TORTS

Negligence

Negligence is probably the most widespread of torts (certainly in relation to actions brought in the courts) and stems from the common law principle that each of us owes a duty of care to anyone whom we might reasonably foresee as being affected by our actions (or omissions). Basically. any breach of that duty of care that results in damage to another person amounts to negligence.

Given that the duty of care exists, the extent of that duty is expressed both as the standard of care and the degree of care. This is where it all gets a little confusing. We all owe the same standard of care, but the degree of care may vary. The standard of care must be that which a reasonable and prudent person would show or expect in the particular circumstances in question. But those who set themselves up as possessing and offering particular skills will owe a higher degree of care than those who do not. If you engage a professional plumber to do some work at your premises, the degree of care that you are entitled to expect of him will be greater than the degree of care than you may expect of your next door neighbour whom you ask to do some plumbing work for you as a favour. But a physiotherapist or osteopath will be expected to display the same *standard* of care in the carrying out of their professions as would a consultant orthopaedic surgeon in carrying out his profession. And incidentally, a learner driver has to show the same *standard* of care to other road users as does an experienced driver.

Negligence applies not only to acts and omissions, it also specifically applies to a negligent misstatement made by, say, an architect, surveyor, solicitor or accountant where a client has acted on negligent advice and suffered damage as a result.

As with contract law and other areas of the common law, parliament has intervened from time to time to enact legislation to extend or modify the common law provisions. Examples are the *Occupier's Liability Act 1957* (which extended the duty of care owed by occupiers of premises to cover all lawful visitors to premises, whether specifically invited or not), and the *Law Reform (Contributory Negligence) Act 1945* (which ended the previous common law situation whereby an alleged wrongdoer could escape all liability by showing that the injured party was to some extent responsible for his own misfortune; liability is now merely reduced accordingly on the basis of, and to the extent of, any 'contributory negligence' on the part of the injured party).

Contributory Negligence
It will be inferred from the immediately preceding paragraph that there is a specific partial defence available in negligence cases - that of contributory negligence. The *Law Reform (Contributory Negligence) Act* already referred to states that:

> Where any person suffers damage as a result partly of his own fault and partly of the fault of any other person or persons, a claim in respect of that damage shall not be defeated by reason of the fault of the person suffering the damage, but the damages recoverable in respect thereof shall be reduced to such an extent as the court thinks just and equitable having regard to the claimant's share in the responsibility for the damage

Remedies and Insurance
The only real remedy for negligence is damages, which can be, and often are, very substantial in personal injury cases. Insurance really is a must for employers, and is compulsory in so far as liability to employees is concerned *(Employer's Liability (Compulsory Insurance) Act 1969)*. Motor insurance for liability to third parties is also compulsory, and public liability for anyone in business is to be highly recommended. (See the section on Business Insurance in Chapter 8)

Nuisance

Public Nuisance and Private Nuisance

A nuisance may be a public nuisance or a private nuisance.

A public nuisance is one that interferes with the safety or comfort of the general public, and may include, for example, disposing of photographic chemicals into the public drains and erecting a tripod and lights on the highway or public footpath. A public nuisance is a criminal offence in addition to being a tort. As a tort, only a person who has suffered damage as a result of the nuisance may sue.

A private nuisance is one that interferes only with certain private rights of an individual as a result of which that individual suffers damage (whether by way of actual material damage, or damage to the peaceful enjoyment of his property or of the normal comforts of life). All sorts of things can amount to a nuisance: noise, smells, vibrations, fumes, smoke, dirt, the obstruction of light, even the roots or branches of a tree. In business terms, operating a business from home may amount to a nuisance if, for example, there are many and frequent visitors to your business premises (particularly in delivery lorries or other vehicles) or if you carry out noisy business activities at weekends or into unsociable hours.

Hounding by Photographer can be a Nuisance

Also, although there is no general right to privacy in English law, a constant or persistent invasion of privacy such as to affect a person's right to peaceful enjoyment of his property might constitute an actionable nuisance. So a press photographer or freelance paparazzo could commit a nuisance if he hounded some famous person or public figure, even if the hounding was carried out from a public highway or other land not belonging to the complainant. The photographer might thereby be liable to damages or an injunction, and if the injunction were breached, the photographer would be in contempt of court and liable to imprisonment.

Remedies for Nuisance

The main remedies for nuisance are damages and injunctions, but there is the additional self-help remedy of 'abatement'. But caution is necessary. You may not enter onto your neighbour's property to 'abate' the nuisance, but you may, for example, cut off the branches and roots of trees that are on, overhanging or under your own property.

Trespass

Three Types of Trespass

Trespass may be to the person, to land, or to goods. In relation to trespass against land or goods, it is the person in lawful occupation or possession who has the rights, not the owner. For example, the owner of freehold land who has granted a lease of that land will not be the lawful 'occupier' of the property; that will be the leaseholder (or perhaps even the holder of a sub-lease or tenancy agreement). With goods, you may lawfully have on your premises goods belonging to another (maybe items brought to you studio for photographing). In such cases, you are in lawful possession of the goods, and you may sue for trespass.

Trespass to the Person

Trespass to the person may be by assault, by battery, or by false imprisonment. 'Battery' is the actual application of physical violence, no matter how slight, whereas 'assault' can be merely the threat of physical violence. 'False imprisonment' does not require actual incarceration: it is the unlawful bodily restraint of another person, howsoever achieved.

Trespass to Land

Trespass to land may be by entry onto that land without the authority of the lawful occupier, by remaining on that land once the authority of the occupier has been revoked, or by depositing any material object on the land without the authority of the occupier.

Photography on and of National Trust and Similar Property

Photography of any property from the public highway does not amount to a trespass; nor does it amount to a breach of privacy (for there is no general law of privacy in English law). The law is that you are free to photograph anything visible from the public highway (or, indeed, from within any adjoining land if you have the authority of the occupier of that land, or unless and until the occupier ejects you from his land). So, by the same token, where a photographer enters onto land or property for the purposes of taking photographs *of* that property, he may only do so with the authority of the occupier (or, in practical terms, until he is caught and ejected if he is photographing against the specific wishes of the occupier).

The occupier of any property may impose such conditions as he chooses on any visitors to the property. And any lawful visitor who breaches those conditions ceases to be a lawful visitor and becomes a trespasser. The National Trust, for instance, has recently banned photography on its property; and so any visitor taking photographs on National Trust property is violating the terms of the 'licence' to be on the property and is therefore a trespasser. As such, he may be ejected from the property, with the use of reasonable force if necessary. However, any photographs that the photographer manages to take before he is caught and asked to leave remain his property and his copyright. The owner of the property has no rights to claim the film(s) or the copyright.

Similarly, many other properties open to the public, apart from National Trust properties, display notices prohibiting the taking of photographs. If those prohibitions are ignored, then the photographer is trespassing. (But beware taking photographs within a theatre or at any other public performance; there will almost certainly be copyright and performing rights implications to consider.)

Trespass to Goods
Trespass to goods is the unlawful interference with goods in the possession of another. The person in possession does not need to be the owner to have a right of action for trespass. Technically, the mere touching of goods can amount to a trespass, but in reality the trespass would need to be more serious than that. So someone who steals your lens or camera is guilty not only of theft but also of trespass to your goods, for which you may sue for damages; and there has also been a trespass if he only 'borrows' the goods without your authority. And if a motor manufacturer client delivers his new model to your studio for photographing and someone steals it, or even just the hubcaps, that is a trespass for which you may sue, even though you are not the owner.

Additional Remedies
If a trespasser to land has been asked peaceably to leave, and, having been given an opportunity to do so, fails to leave, the occupier may invoke his own remedy of ejecting the trespasser, provided, of course, that any physical force used is proportionate and reasonable (otherwise the occupier will himself become guilty of the torts of assault and battery). Alternatively, the occupier may apply to the court to order the ejection of a trespasser.

Conversion

The tort of conversion is the wrongful and unlawful interference with goods belonging to another person, inconsistent with the rights of that other person to the use and possession of the goods. The wronged party may sue for monetary damages or, where appropriate and where the goods are still in existence and in the possession of the wrongdoer, for the discretionary remedy, of 'specific delivery' (an order of the court that the goods shall be returned).

Breach of Statutory Duty

Breach of a statutory duty is itself a tort, and gives rise to the right to sue for damages, injunctions and all of the usual appropriate remedies.

Infringement of the moral rights under the terms of the *Copyright, Designs and Patents Act 1988* is a breach of statutory duty, as are failures to uphold and adhere to the responsibilities laid down by the *Health and Safety at Work Act 1974*. (See, respectively, Chapter 5 - PHOTOGRAPHIC COPYRIGHT and Chapter 4 - EMPLOYMENT LAW)

Libel and Slander

Definitions and Distinctions

Libel and slander both come under the broader heading of 'defamation', which is defined as 'the publication of any false statement which exposes a person to hatred, ridicule or contempt or which causes him generally to be shunned or avoided by right-thinking members of society'. In more modern parlance, this means any untrue statement which damages a person's reputation.

The important points to note about the definition are that *(a)* 'publication' merely means showing or speaking the statement to any single third party (it does not have to be 'published' in the sense of being printed in a publication); *(b)* that 'statement' includes a photograph and also that it includes a statement by innuendo; *(c)* that the statement must be untrue; *(d)* that it must identifiably refer to the complainant; and *(e)* that it must be such as to discredit him. Also note that it is not only the originator of the statement who is liable; anyone involved in the repetition, dissemination or distribution of the libel is equally liable. Hence when the British Institute of Professional Photography initiated libel proceedings in 1989 arising out of an article published in the *Master Photographer* magazine, the BIPP issued writs against the author of the article, the editor of the magazine, the publishing company that owned the magazine, and the printers of the magazine. (That case was settled out of court by a full retraction of the offending article, the issue of a public apology, and the payment of all of the BIPP's legal costs by the publishing company and the author of the article, and the writs against all parties were withdrawn.)

The main distinctions between libel and slander are *(a)* that libel is the publication of such a statement in permanent form (including, under the provisions of the *Defamation Act 1952*, by way of a radio or television broadcast), whereas slander is publication in transitory form (that is, by speech), and *(b)* that a person claiming to have been the subject of slander must prove that he has suffered actual damage (except in cases of allegations of certain criminal behaviour, infection by a contagious disease, lack of chastity of a woman, and unfitness for the person's office, profession or business), whereas a person claiming to have been libelled merely needs to prove publication of the libel and that the libel referred to him, whether or not actual damage resulted.

Both libel and slander, unusually for civil cases, are tried before a judge *and jury* in the High Court, leading to very high legal costs. The amount of damages is determined by the jury and not by the judge, and also tends to be high, as some celebrated or notorious cases in recent years have demonstrated.

Defences to Libel
The main defences against a libel action are:

- Justification
- Fair Comment
- Privilege

Justification
This amounts to the offender sticking to his guns and saying that the statement was essentially true. It is a dangerous defence to use if the offender is not sure of his grounds. The onus is on him to prove that it is true, and if the jury decides in the end that it was not true, the offender may be penalised by substantial punitive damages. (It is not a libel to say

or publish something that is true, no matter how damaging it may be to the person(s) concerned.)

Fair Comment

In relation to matters of public interest or in relation to people in public life, the offender can argue that the statement published amounted to 'fair comment'. Note that people in public life does not mean 'famous people'; it actually means what it says - people in public life. Note also that a matter of public interest does not mean matters that are of interest to the public; the two are very different. The private life of a pop star might be of interest to the public, but it is not a matter of public interest. Broadly speaking, a matter of public interest should concern a matter of public policy, or matters that are legitimately within the public domain, such as published works of art and public performances.

For the defence of fair comment to succeed, the statement must consist of the speaker's or writer's genuine and honestly held opinion; it must not be a statement of fact, and it must not be tainted by malice or some other improper motive.

Privilege

There are two forms of privilege: absolute privilege and qualified privilege. Absolute privilege covers parliamentary and judicial proceedings (including any statements made by witnesses giving evidence to parliamentary committees or to proceedings in a court). Qualified privilege includes fair and accurate reports of parliamentary and judicial proceedings, and communications between a solicitor and his client (though some legal authorities suggest that this may be a case of absolute privilege). Absolute privilege is a defence to any action for libel or slander. Qualified privilege provides a defence provided there is no malice and the statement was honestly believed to be true. Where malice is proved, the defence of qualified privilege is withdrawn and the offender will be held liable for the libel (or slander).

Libel by Photography

Given that one of the essential characteristics of a libel is that it is untrue, can a photograph ever be libellous? The answer to that is 'yes', but usually only because of the context in which it is published or in conjunction with a caption. (The scope for libel by photography is enhanced considerably by modern electronic methods of image manipulation. But for comments on this, please see Chapter 9 - THE NEW TECH-NOLOGIES.) For now, let us concentrate on libel by 'conventional' photography.

Two particular reported cases might help us to understand how a photograph can be libellous (and remember that a libel can be by innuendo).

The first case is that of *Cassidy v The Daily Mirror [1929]*. A Daily Mirror photographer, attending a race meeting at Aintree, photographed a Mr Michael Cassidy with a lady friend. The picture was published with a caption that said Mr Cassidy and the lady friend had announced their engagement. This was not true, and Mr Cassidy was in fact already married (albeit separated). Mr Cassidy's wife sued the Daily Mirror, pleading that the innuendo was that she was not really Mr Cassidy's wife but his mistress. She won the case and was awarded damages.

The case of *Tolley v Fry [1931]* concerned a prominent amateur golfer who had been pictured with a bar of Fry's chocolate visible in his pocket. Without Mr Tolley's authority or knowledge, the picture was used by Fry's in an advertising campaign, and Mr Tolley sued on the basis that it suggested that he had compromised his amateur status by accepting money for product endorsement. Mr Tolley won his case; the picture (with accompanying words) was held to be libellous. But it is very likely that, even without any words, that picture would have been libellous in the context in which it was used. Fashions change in advertising, and it is perfectly possible to imagine that kind of picture being used today without any words at all; the picture says it all.

Photographers really must take the greatest of care in the uses to which they allow their photographs to be put, and also (where it is their responsibility) in the wording of any captions. But it does not end there. Let us imagine one or two hypothetical cases that could easily happen (and may already have happened). You are doing some glamour photography on location; or it may even be some fashion or commercial photography. You photograph a scantily-clad woman, and in the background is the identifiable stately home of a prominent politician; perhaps even a member of the cabinet. The photograph was actually taken on a neighbouring property. The photograph is subsequently published, and people assume that our prominent politician has given his authority for such goings-on on his property, that he condones semi-naked women on his property, or even that he is profiting from it. Almost without the shadow of a doubt, that would amount to a libel.

And what if you were to photograph a man, any man, who just happens to be a teetotaller, a fact well known to his friends and associates. Maybe you have never even met the man; it could be a candid street shot. And what if you photographed him just as he was passing a pub, just as he accidentally tripped over an uneven paving stone, and just as he put out his hand to steady himself against the pub wall? That photograph would probably give the impression that the man was staggering drunk! If published, that picture would almost certainly be libellous. And remember that to 'publish' in the context of libel merely means showing it, or allowing it to be seen, by one other person.

Model Releases

Given the gist of the previous few paragraphs, this is as good a place as any within this book to comment on the use of Model Release Forms. (The subject of Model Releases could equally have appeared in the sections on the contractual relationships of commercial and editorial photographers; and some people confuse it with copyright - with which it has no connection whatsoever.) The importance of gaining the authority of any models for the use of their images cannot be over-stressed; indeed it would also apply to the use of a person's identifiable property or props. Standard Model Release Forms are available from the Association of Photographers and the British Institute of Professional Photography. But you can just as easily devise your own.

A Model Release Form should *(a)* identify the photographer and the model; *(b)* refer to the date(s) of the photography in question, *(c)* as accurately as possible refer to or describe the photography in question so as to identify it; *(d)* specify the anticipated or permitted use(s) to which the photography will be put; and *(e)* (to take the words directly from the BIPP Model Release Form) carry the signature of the model to words to the following effect:

> In consideration of the sum of £*[blank]* and any other sums which may become due to me, and conditionally upon payment of the aforesaid sums and the undertaking of the Photographer given below, I permit the Photographer and his licensees or assignees to use the photograph(s) referred to above and/or drawings therefrom and any

other reproductions or adaptations thereof either complete or in part, alone or in conjunction with any wording and/or drawings solely and exclusively for . . .

and then it gives a number of tick boxes relating to the agreed use(s), and it continues:

I understand that such material shall be deemed to represent an imaginary person unless otherwise agreed in writing by me or my agent. I understand that I do not own the copyright in the photograph(s)

followed, of course by the model's signature. The 'undertaking of the Photographer' referred to merely says that the material shall be used only in accordance with the terms of the Release.

Some advertising agency clients will insist on there being a Model Release before they will use an image. Editorial clients ought to too.

Privacy Generally

There is no general law of privacy in English Law. In the context of the law relating to photography, that means that a citizen has no legal right to object to his photograph being taken, and, once his image is taken (whether with or without his authority) he has no right to prohibit any particular use of that image.

However, this general statement of the legal position must be regarded in the light of possible considerations of trespass (where, for example, it is necessary to enter on to private property in order to take the photograph), considerations of libel (in relation to how and in what context the photograph is published), and in the light of certain prohibitions and restrictions on photography as outlined in the following chapter (relating mainly to judicial proceedings and contempt of court).

CHAPTER SEVEN

LEGAL RESTRICTIONS ON PHOTOGRAPHY

OBSCENE AND INDECENT PHOTOGRAPHS

In the area of obscenity, there are three main acts of parliament that could result in criminal prosecutions of photographers and those who handle or deal in photography.

The Obscene Publications Act 1959

The Obscene Publications Act 1959 makes it a criminal offence, punishable by an unlimited fine or up to three years' imprisonment, for any person, whether for gain or not, to publish an obscene article or to possess an obscene article for publication or gain (although it was always a common law offence even prior to the passing of the Act). The Act defines 'obscene article' as follows:

> An article shall be deemed to be obscene if its effect is such as to tend to deprave and corrupt persons who are likely, having regard to all relevant circumstances, to read, see or hear the matter contained or embodied in it

An 'article' includes a photograph, of course; 'publish' (in the first paragraph) includes distributing, lending, circulating, selling, giving, hiring, and offering for sale or hire; and 'obscenity' is not limited to material of a sexually explicit nature but includes depictions of violence too. And incidentally, it is no defence to say that a particular photograph cannot corrupt or deprave people because the people to whom it is shown are already corrupt and depraved!

What amounts to 'corrupt' and 'deprave' is subjective; different magistrates and different juries will take different views. And, of course, social attitudes change over time, and this will be reflected in changing interpretations of the Act. One of the first prosecutions under the Act was the celebrated case against Penguin Books Ltd in 1960 for publishing the formerly-censored D. H. Lawrence novel, *Lady Chatterley's Lover*. It is not necessary to go over the history of that case in this book, but thankfully the jury at the time had the good sense to reject some of the nonsense and pompous arguments of the prosecution and acquit Penguin Books. The point, though, is that it is impossible to imagine such a prosecution even being contemplated today: and, given the number of lurid and explicit magazines that have not been prosecuted and which are on sale now in the average newsagent's shop, that is a measure of the change in social attitudes over the intervening decades.

But the bottom line for photographers remains that the Act is still there; there are still many circumstances in which it is invoked; and, ultimately, the prospect is still there of a three-year stretch!

The Protection of Children Act 1978

Although obscene photographs of children are covered by the *Obscene Publications Act*, the *Protection of Children Act 1978* goes further, in that it makes it an offence to take an 'indecent' photograph of a child. It is far easier, of course, for the prosecuting authorities to obtain convictions in cases involving the lesser element of 'indecency' than in cases of alleged 'obscenity'. And it is not only the *taking* of an indecent photograph of a child that constitutes an offence under the Act; it is also an offence to distribute or show such a photograph, or even to possess it with a view to distributing or showing it to another.

The level at which a photograph may be held to be 'indecent' is quite low. In 1992, a professional photographer in his 60s, of previous good character and with over 30 years' standing as a professional, was convicted of taking an indecent photograph of a child (an eight-year-old girl) when, at the request of the child's mother, he made a video film of a day in the child's life and included a scene of the child in, and emerging from, the shower. (The child later mentioned it to her aunt who then alerted the authorities.) The photographer in question did not go to jail, but was severely embarrassed and suffered damage to his business as a result of the publicity.

The maximum penalties on conviction are the same as for the 'obscenity' offences mentioned earlier.

The Post Office Act 1953

It is an offence under the *Post Office Act 1953* to send indecent or obscene material through the post. The maximum penalty in this case is 12 months' imprisonment or a fine.

For the purposes of this Act only, the Act itself defines what amounts to indecent or obscene as material that is 'grossly offensive or of an indecent or obscene character'. Note that this is far less a burden for the prosecuting authorities to prove than actually being 'obscene'. For this reason, many mail order D&P labs will sometimes refuse to return certain processed films and prints through the post (and understandably so) and instead will contact the customer and ask him to collect them in person.

The difference in the levels of the burden of proof between the *Obscene Publications Act* and the *Post Office Act* was admirably demonstrated in the case of *R v Anderson [1974]*. Anderson had been convicted of offences under both Acts, but on appeal, the conviction under the *Post Office Act* was upheld whereas the conviction under the *Obscene Publications Act* was quashed.

PHOTOGRAPHY OF COURTS AND LEGAL PROCEEDINGS

The photographer should be aware of a number of points relating to photography in and around court buildings and to photography relating to legal proceedings.

The Judicial Proceedings (Regulations and Reports) Act 1926

Section 1 of the *Judicial Proceedings (Regulations and Reports) Act 1926* prohibits the publication of any indecent material that is produced in evidence in court proceedings:

> It shall not be lawful to print or publish, or cause to be printed or published, in relation to any judicial proceedings any indecent matter or indecent medical, surgical or psychological details, the publication of which would be calculated to injure public morals

Photography of Persons in Court

It is a criminal offence under Section 41(1) of the *Criminal Justice Act 1925* to take any photograph within a court or to publish any such photograph, by whomsoever taken:

> No person shall (a) take or attempt to take in any court any photograph . . . . of any person, being a judge of the court, or a juror or a witness in, or a party to, any proceedings before the court, whether civil or criminal, or (b) publish any photograph . . . . taken or made in contravention of this section, or any reproduction thereof

For the purposes of this Section, 'in any court' is deemed to include any area within the court building and also the precincts and curtilage of the building. Strictly speaking, therefore, many offences are committed everyday, as we often see, in newspapers and on the television news, pictures of relevant persons entering or leaving a court building. However, if you are involved or likely to be involved in this type of photography, just be aware that it is actually a criminal offence; and prudence dictates that you do not actually photograph the judge or the magistrate(s)! And bear in mind also that the same provisions of the Act will apply in cases where a court goes out 'on location' to hear or examine particular evidence.

Contempt of Court

One area of the law where justice can be remarkably swift is contempt of court: and the punishments can be harsh!

The concept of contempt of court has existed for a very long time at common law, and is based on the principle that nobody should undermine the integrity of the law or of the courts or seek to obstruct or interfere with the independent administration of justice. Parliament sought to codify the common law of contempt by enacting the *Contempt of Court Act 1981*, but certain aspects of the common law remain (and, indeed, have been considerably extended even since the passing of the Act).

Pre-Trial Publicity

At common law, a person is guilty of an offence if he publishes, or causes to be published, any material (including photographs, of course) calculated to interfere with judicial proceedings which are 'imminent or pending' at the time of publication. One of the major common law precedents for this is a 1927 case involving the *Daily Mirror*, which published a picture of an accused man on the day that he was to appear on an identity parade. One of the appeal judges in the case declared that:

> *There is a duty to refrain from publication of a photograph where it is apparent to a reasonable man that a question of identity arises*

Contempt of Court Act 1981

In criminal cases, 'imminent or pending' under the old common law usually meant after an arrest had been made but before the trial had commenced; but that was not invariably so. The difficulty, particularly for photographers, journalists and their editors, was how to know if proceedings were 'imminent or pending' or how to know if an arrest had actually been made. The *Contempt of Court Act 1981* sought to clarify the position using the concept of 'proceedings being active' and by defining that quite tightly. But even since the passing of the Act, the courts have upheld the old common law as still subsisting, and have even considerably extended its scope in one notable case involving *The Sun* newspaper, where 'imminent and pending' was held to have applied seven weeks *prior* to an arrest having been made. So the aim of the 1981 Act to clarify the position has failed, and photographers, journalists and editors are probably even less sure now of their position than they were before!

Identity of an Accused Person

So far as most photographers are concerned, though, the main issue is the taking of any photograph of an accused person in any case in which identity is, or is likely to be, a key issue. The best advice can only be: if in doubt, don't.

Other Persons not to be Identified

Identity of a Victim of Rape or Associated Offences

Not a contempt of court, but a separate offence of its own under the *Sexual Offences(Amendment) Act 1976*, as amended by the *Criminal Justice Act 1988*, is the publication of the identity of, or of any matter likely to lead the public to be able to identify (including a still or moving picture), any woman who has made a complaint of any of the following offences:

- Rape;
- Attempted rape;
- Aiding or abetting rape or attempted rape;
- Inciting, counselling or procuring rape;
- Conspiracy to rape; and
- Burglary with intent to rape.

Note that the prohibition does not, therefore, extend to complaints of other sexual offences.

No offence is committed under these provisions if the woman concerned gives her consent to the publication of her identity. Moreover, the provisions against publication last for the lifetime of the woman. Therefore there is no legal restriction on publication of the woman's identity if she was the victim of rape *and* murder.

Identity of Juveniles

In cases in the Juvenile Courts, it is an offence to publish any matter that could lead to the identification of a juvenile defendant or a juvenile witness *(Children and Young Persons Act 1933)*. A juvenile is a person under the age of 17. The offence would be committed by anyone publishing any photograph by which the juvenile might be identified. This would include publication of any picture (associated with any reference to the case) of the young person's school or of any identifiable teacher or relative; in fact anything by which the young person may be identified.

PHOTOGRAPHY AT PUBLIC INCIDENTS
AND DEMONSTRATIONS

General

Subject to the laws of trespass (for which see Chapter 6), a photographer is fully entitled to take photographs at any public meeting or demonstration or at the scene of any incident. However, it is an offence under the *Highways Act 1959* for any person wilfully and without lawful authority to obstruct free passage along a highway, and police officers have powers of arrest in cases of threatening behaviour, breach of the peace, or obstruction of a police officer in the execution of his duty. So discretion and common sense must prevail.

Specific Offences

Breach of the Peace

Any person who, in any public place, uses threatening, abusive or insulting words or behaviour with intent to provoke a breach of the peace or whereby a breach of the peace is likely to occur is guilty of an offence under either the *Metropolitan Police Act 1839* (within the Metropolitan Police area) or the *Public Order Act 1936* (which extended the same provisions to the whole of England and Wales, including the Metropolitan Police area). It is easy to see how a police officer at a rowdy demonstration or at a major incident or disaster could become irritated by the activities of a persistent photographer, and how easy it is for the photographer to make a nuisance of himself in the eyes of the police officer. If such a situation degenerates into verbal abuse or physical jostling, the police officer would probably imagine that he has good grounds to arrest the photographer and have him carted off in a police van. Whether or not the police officer actually had good grounds is a matter for the photographer to argue before the magistrates the following day. But by then it's too late; the photographer will have lost the opportunity to get his pictures. It is better, therefore, to try to keep the situation calm in the first place, and not to do anything that is likely to provoke the police officer. After all, the object is to get some pictures, not to spend the night in a cell!

Obstruction of a Police Officer

Many of the observations made above apply equally in the case of obstructing a police officer in the execution of his duty (an offence under *Police Act 1964*). To 'obstruct' in this context does not refer merely to physical obstruction, but to any behaviour calculated to make it more difficult for the police officer to do his job.

Confiscation of Film or Camera

There is no law that gives a police officer or any other person the right to confiscate or wilfully damage a photographer's film or camera when taking pictures at a demonstration or major incident. Any such interference with a person's property amounts to a trespass to goods (see Chapter 6 for appropriate remedies, but there is the great difficulty of assessing and proving the actual extent of any financial loss that may have been suffered as a result of any such interference).

Police Powers of Search and Seizure

Does a police officer have the power to search your premises to seize your camera or film if he suspects that it contains evidence relating to a crime? The basic answer is 'no, he does not', unless he first obtains a warrant. Under the *Police and Criminal Evidence Act 1984*, a search warrant may be granted by a magistrate if a police officer has reasonable grounds to believe that:

1. a 'serious arrestable offence' has been committed (as may well be the case at demonstrations and major incidents);
2. that there is material on the specified premises that is likely to be of substantial value to the investigation of an offence (which your photographs might well be);
3. that the material is likely to be admissible evidence (which photographs generally are); and
4. that it is not material to which special privileges or exclusions apply (which photographs may or may not be - see below).

If you are a good citizen and have no particular reason to deny the police access to the material, then you might as well consent and hand it over, because if the relevant conditions listed above all apply, the officer will almost certainly get his warrant anyway. However, if your photographs were taken by you as a journalist (which includes photojournalist), then you may want to resist handing them over to the police, or at least not be seen to do so voluntarily, in order to protect your professional integrity and independence. The Act then gives you a better chance of resisting seizure, as journalistic material comes under the heading of 'special procedure material', which necessitates the police officer obtaining a warrant from a judge rather than from a magistrate, and also gives you the right to be notified in advance of the application and the right to oppose the application in front of the judge.

WILDLIFE PHOTOGRAPHY

There are various legal restrictions on the photography of wildlife, mainly as prescribed in the *Wildlife and Countryside Act 1981*. In many cases, photography is not, of itself, illegal, but it is necessary first to obtain a licence. This applies particularly in the case of rare breeding birds. There are penalties (usually fines) for carrying on a particular activity without having obtained a licence, and the granting of licences is certainly not automatic. The licensing authority will need to be assured of a person's relevant expertise and integrity. For information about licences, you should contact the Royal Society for the Protection of Birds or English Nature (formerly the Nature Conservancy Council), both of whose addresses are given at Appendix 5 at the end of this book.

Birds

There are no restrictions on photographing the most common species of bird (for example, crows, sparrows, gulls, pigeons, starlings, magpies and the like), but there is a great list of wild birds that are protected, either throughout the year or at nesting times. Any photographer wanting full details of the restrictions and the species of birds affected is advised to contact the Royal Society for the Protection of Birds or English Nature.

Other Species

There are also many other species of wildlife that enjoy protection of sorts, including varieties of otter, toad, butterfly, bat, red squirrel, dolphin, moth, snail and spider. Similarly, licences must be obtained to photograph these species in their natural habitats. For further details, contact English Nature.

Plants

Licences are not required to photograph the many varieties and species of protected plant life, but anyone with an interest in photographing them should be aware that picking, uprooting or otherwise destroying them is in many cases prohibited. Where it is permitted, a licence will usually be required.

CHAPTER EIGHT

TRADING STATUS AND BUSINESS INSURANCE

TRADING STATUS

One of the earliest and most important decisions to be made when contemplating starting in business is the 'status' of your trading unit. Will you opt to trade as an incorporated limited company or as a self-employed, sole trader? Or if you are going into business with a partner, will it be as a limited company or as an unincorporated partnership?

Having once made the decision, it might be that you will revise your decision after a few years' trading, perhaps because of expansion, or maybe on the advice of your accountant or tax adviser because of certain tax advantages to be gained.

Limited Company

To trade as a limited company is certainly the most bureaucratic and regulated of the choices on offer. A limited company is a company formally incorporated under the *Companies Act 1985*. When a company is formed, it acquires a legal status of its own; it becomes a legal entity, entirely distinct from the identity of its shareholders and directors. A company may sue and be sued in its own name, just like a natural person, and a company can commit, be charged with, and convicted of, a criminal offence. A company cannot go to jail, of course, but it can be heavily fined. In short, a company is a legal person.

Limited Liability

The essence of a limited company is that the liability of its members (its shareholders) is limited to the amount of money paid or pledged to be paid to buy the shares. So that, in theory at least, once a company is formed (and it may be formed with a share capital of as little as £100), if the company subsequently fails, the shareholders will not be liable for the debts of the company. However, it rarely works like that! In most small companies, the shareholders are also the directors, and there are quite severe penalties now for directors who mismanage the affairs of a company and who continue the trading of the company knowing it to be insolvent. Moreover, it is almost impossible to get finance for a small company (by way of loans and bank overdrafts) without the banks wanting *personal* guarantees from the directors, so overriding their limited liability as shareholders. A company must have at least two shareholders. In many small, family companies, the only shareholders are the husband and wife. The shares may be split between them in any way they wish; say 50% each, or 99% to one party and 1% to the other party, or even all shares but one being owned by one party and the one remaining share being held by the other.

Insolvency

A company is technically insolvent if it is unable to pay its debts as they fall due or if its liabilities exceed its assets. And, as suggested earlier, directors who allow a company to continue to trade whilst insolvent are committing a serious criminal offence.

Directors and Company Secretary

Although a company may have only two shareholders, the minimum number of directors is only one. However, a company must also have a company secretary, and a person who is a sole director may not also be the company secretary. (The company secretary does not have to be a director of the company.)

The *Companies Act* places very onerous duties and responsibilities on directors and company secretaries. Indeed the Act contains over 140 criminal offences that a director or company secretary may commit! These range from fraudulent trading and false accounting, through the trading whilst insolvent provisions already referred to, to failing to file forms and returns accurately or on time.

At all times, the overriding duty of a director (both individually and collectively with his fellow directors) is to act in the best interests of the company. This has been held by the courts to mean in the best interests of the shareholders; the employees are not the directors' first concern.

Note that a director is technically an employee of the company; he is not self-employed. This applies even if he is the majority shareholder and the sole director. As such, the company must account for his income tax and Class 1 National Insurance contributions monthly under the PAYE system, just as for any other employee. He may take profits out of the company by way of a dividend on his shares, but that is a different matter; so far as his salary or regular drawings are concerned, he is regarded as the same as any other employee. Incidentally, a director is not entitled to take anything out of the company other than his salary, pension contributions, repayments of loans made to the company and any declared dividends on shares. Remember that a company is a separate legal person, and as such it owns property entirely separately from its directors. The property of a company is *not* the property of any individual shareholder or director.

The company itself is liable to corporation tax on its profits.

Memorandum and Articles of Association

The first bureaucracy associated with a company is in its formation and registration. The company must have a Memorandum of Association and Articles of Association. The Memorandum of Association lays down the objects for which the company was (or is being) formed. It is usual to draft the objects of a company fairly widely, and to include a clause such as '. . . and to do any other things incidental and conducive thereto as the directors shall in their absolute discretion consider to be in the interests of the company'. A company may only do something that it is empowered to do by its Memorandum. Any act outside of those powers is void, and the directors may find themselves personally liable.

The Articles of Association lay down the rules governing the internal management of the company. A company can either draw up its own Articles of Association or, if it chooses not to, standard Articles published within the *Companies Act* will apply.

The Memorandum and Articles of Association amount to the constitution of a company, and every aspect of a company's internal management and external dealings must be conducted strictly in accordance with the Memorandum and Articles.

Company Name

A company must have a name, which must always finish with the word 'limited' (or its Welsh equivalent) or the letters 'plc' (public limited company) in the case of a public company. We are not really concerned with public limited companies. Most small companies are what is known as 'private' or 'close' companies. A company that exists for charitable purposes or that is a professional institute, for example, may apply for dispensation not to use the word 'limited' in its title; but it remains a limited company none the less.

A company name must be unique, in that you cannot register a company with the same name as another company already registered. Nor will you be allowed to use any name that implies royal or government patronage or that implies officialdom or national or international standing. For example, words like 'British', 'royal', 'national', 'council', 'committee', 'institute' and 'authority' will not be permitted.

Annual Audit, Accounts and Report

There are strict and stringent accountancy rules for limited companies, including the requirement for the company's accounts to be audited by a qualified person at least once a year. The accounts (being a statement of income and expenditure for the year plus a balance sheet made up as at the last day of the accounting period) must be submitted to Companies House annually (along with the Annual Report of the directors). Additionally, there is a requirement to hold annual general meetings of the company and to keep proper minutes of these and of meetings of the directors.

Company Name on Stationery and at Premises

All company letterheads, invoices and statements must carry the full name of the company (including the word 'limited'), the address of the registered office of the company (which may or may not be the place from where the company operates; it may be the address of your accountant or solicitor), and the registration number of the company. There is no compulsion to show the names of directors on company letterheads, but if the name of one director is shown, then the names of all directors must be shown.

The name of a company must be prominently displayed outside every premises from which the company operates.

So Why Start a Company?

A very good question! Frankly, it can only be for one of four reasons: because of certain tax advantages in individual cases (but that is a matter for professional advice from a specialist adviser); because rapid expansion is planned or expected and it would be imprudent to have the unlimited liability of a self-employed sole trader; because a 'partnership' of sorts is intended and there is a need or desire to avoid all of the risks associated with an unincorporated partnership; or because of some perverted ego!

Self-Employed Sole Trader

Most people starting up in business opt to trade as self-employed sole traders. This certainly avoids much of the horrendous bureaucracy associated with companies, but it does expose the sole trader to unlimited liability, to the full extent of his assets, in the event of the business running into financial difficulties.

All the property of the business is the property of the trader, for there is no separate legal entity as with a company. The personal affairs and assets of the sole trader are indivisible from the affairs and assets of his business.

A sole trader accounts for his income, expenditure and profits each year to the Inland Revenue, and his tax is assessed accordingly. He does not have to account monthly to the Inland Revenue for income tax and National Insurance under the PAYE system. The sole trader pays regular Class 2 National Insurance contributions at whatever is the current rate, and then additional Class 4 contributions at a later date dependent upon the amount of profits the business makes.

A sole trader may trade under his own name in isolation (as, for example, in W. Higgs or William Higgs) or under any other name (such as William Higgs Photography, Higgs Studios, or Sunrise Photographics) provided that it does not infringe the rights of the owner of a registered trade mark or amount to 'passing off' (see page 64 in chapter 5). Where a trader trades under a name other than his own name in isolation, the name of the trader has to be disclosed to anyone who may wish to know it.

When first starting in business as a self-employed sole trader, it is important to make early contact with your current (or immediate past) Inspector of Taxes and with the local office of the Department of Social Security, so as to ensure that all of your tax and National Insurance affairs are properly in order.

Partnership

It has been said that you need to be even more careful when choosing a business partner than when choosing a marriage partner. That is sound advice! (And it also applies, though to a lesser degree, when you start a limited company with a 'partner'.)

In this context of partnership, though, we are talking about an unincorporated partnership; that is, a partnership that is not a limited company. A business partnership is two (or more, generally up to a maximum of 20) self-employed people trading together as one entity. And there are dangers and pitfalls by the score! It is easy to be wise after the event, but there are many thousands of ex-partners who wish they had given more thought to their partnerships at the start. Seek professional advice. Go to a solicitor, and ask him to draw up a 'deed of partnership' that outlines (nay, *details*) the duties, responsibilities and liabilities of each partner to the other(s), and which clearly spells out the relationship between the partners. What if one partner becomes incapacitated? What if one partner dies? What if one partner's work is not up to scratch, or he is not pulling his weight? Who will be authorised to spend money and to sign cheques? What if you simply fall out and cannot stand the sight of each other? All of these things (and more) really ought to be thought about and ironed out *before* you commit yourself to a partnership. This really cannot be over-emphasised! If no deed of partnership is entered into, then the terms of the *Partnership Act 1890* will apply in default.

Why all the scare stories? Well, let's look at the facts. Every partner is fully and jointly liable for all of the debts and liabilities of the partnership, up to the maximum extent of his assets (as with the self-employed sole trader). But if the partnership fails (with debts, let's say, of £50,000 - a fairly modest figure in modern business terms) any creditor can choose to seek recompense in full from any one of the partners; he does not have to sue each partner for an equal share. It is then up to the partner sued to try to get money from the other partner(s). And there is worse. Every partner is liable to pay his own income tax and National Insurance contributions, but if any partner(s) should fail to do so, the Inland Revenue may come to the remaining partner(s) instead!

Having read all of this, perhaps you now agree with the comment at the beginning of this section about being more careful choosing business partners than marriage partners. Often, of course, the marriage partner also becomes a business partner. The consequences of that are truly horrendous if the marriage breaks up, as so often and sadly it does. In summary, professional legal advice is an absolute must before going into any business partnership.

BUSINESS INSURANCE

At various points throughout this book reference is made to the importance of insurance for different types of business risks. The following are the main business insurances that the prudent photographer will wish to consider. However, once again it has to be recommended that expert professional advice is sought; and remember that insurance brokers do not charge fees or commissions.

Employer's Liability Insurance

This is mentioned first, mainly because, along with motor insurance, it is the only insurance that is compulsory. It is compulsory under the terms of the *Employer's Liability (Compulsory Insurance) Act 1969* for any business that employs anyone other than members of the employer's own immediate family. Remember, though, that if you are the director of a limited company, then the company employs you; the company therefore has employees. A copy of the certificate of insurance must be displayed on every premises at which the business operates.

Employer's Liability Insurance covers the risks of injury to employees in the course of their employment, for which the employer is usually liable. The very minimum level of cover recommended is £1,000,000 for any single event.

Public Liability Insurance

This is very similar to Employer's Liability Insurance except that it is to cover your liability for damage or injury to members of the public (who may be your clients and other lawful visitors to your premises). Public Liability is not compulsory, but no prudent business will be without it. Damages for personal injury claims can run into hundreds of thousands of pounds, and if you or your company are found liable, the consequences of inadequate insurance cover might be liquidation and personal bankruptcy. Again, the minimum cover should be at least £1,000,000 for any single incident.

Motor Insurance

We all know about motor insurance, of course, and we all accept the need for it (although the need for other forms of insurance is often just as great, and yet not so readily accepted). Motor insurance is the other mandatory insurance cover, and fully comprehensive cover has to be preferred to just third party, fire and theft cover.

Professional Indemnity Insurance

Professional Indemnity Insurance is to cover your liability to clients for any failure on your part to fulfil your contractual obligations, whether as a result of your own negligence or recklessness or as a result of matters beyond your control such as a disaster at your lab or an undetectable camera fault (or, if your business is a photographic laboratory, to cover your liability to your photographer clients for any failure in your lab). The maximum amount of cover need not be high, and depends on the type of work you do. Cover for a maximum of £10,000 for any one incident, with a maximum cover of £50,000 in any single year, should be more than enough. The premiums can often be high for professional indemnity insurance, as there is a very limited market of companies willing to offer the cover. And if you accumulate a poor record of claims, the new premium at renewal time will probably be prohibitive.

Libel Insurance

Insurance against the risks of facing (and losing) libel actions is available, but as with professional indemnity insurance, the market is very limited. Most photographers will not find it appropriate, but if you actually produce a publication or if you work in a high risk area of photography, you ought to consider it.

Buildings and Contents Insurance

This is the bread and butter of business insurances, and the level of cover required will obviously vary from business to business. The level of premiums is likely to vary, too, dependent, among other things, upon your geographical location. There is always a serious danger of under-insurance, and it is advisable to have a regular review of your insurance needs, adding in the value of new equipment that you might have acquired. Study the terms of your policy very carefully; you may actually be required to notify the insurance company of specific details of any high value equipment, including serial numbers.

All-Risks Insurance

Photographers' all-risks policies are available from a number of sources. 'All-risks' does not actually mean all-risks; basically it is a combined policy for buildings and contents insurance and public and employer's liability insurances. It certainly will not include either professional indemnity insurance or libel insurance.

Insurance - Contracts of 'Utmost Good Faith'

Any contract for insurance is known as a contract of the 'utmost good faith'. What this means is that a policy holder, or a prospective policy holder, has a duty to disclose any material facts, whether the insurance company specifically asks for them or not. Failure to disclose any material fact might enable the insurer to avoid liability in the event of a claim.

CHAPTER NINE

THE NEW TECHNOLOGIES

LEGAL AND ETHICAL CONSIDERATIONS

Introduction

This short chapter does not contain any substantive points of law that have not already been covered elsewhere within this book. Rather, it is intended as a brief comment upon the implications of some of the rapidly advancing technologies available to photographers and users of photographic images. It probably poses more questions than it answers and, sadly, will come to the conclusion that the law is incapable of providing adequate protection of photographers and their rights in the context of the new and yet-to-emerge technologies.

Photography is probably unique in the degree to which it spans the entire spectrum of human interest and activity from fine art to applied science. At the latter extreme, for example, we use photography, and take photography for granted, in medicine, forensic science, industrial research, aerial survey, and space exploration; at the other extreme, photography may have no other purpose than to hang on our walls as articles of adornment. In between, there is a myriad of everyday applications from advertising through to weddings.

Photography Defined

The word 'photography' is derived from Greek, and merely means 'light drawing'. There is nothing in the definition of photography that restricts or limits it to a chemical process. The fact that the recording medium might be a CCD chip or some other electronic device, rather than a silver halide emulsion, does not negate the use of the word photography. Nor is the distinction between moving and still images relevant: a moving image is only an optical illusion based on a series of still images. If the foregoing is accepted, then electronic photography has been a reality for over half a century: it is called television!

Misuses and Abuses

None the less, recent developments in the technologies available and used in photography, particularly in relation to the 'still' image, have led to some concern about possible misuses and abuses. Broadly, these concerns are based on three factors. First, there is the ease with which images can be created digitally, or subsequently digitised, and thereafter reproduced infinitely with no picture degradation. Secondly, there is the ability to manipulate an image electronically, again with no picture degradation, and with a subsequent viewer of the image being totally unaware that any manipulation has taken place. And thirdly, there is the ease of global transmission of digital images, almost instantaneously, and still with no picture degradation. Although it is easy to see how the unscrupulous will take advantage of these developments, it is important to welcome them as major, positive steps in the advancement of photography and information technology.

To relate the above three factors specifically to the relevant areas of law necessitates consideration of, at the very least, the copyright aspects, libel, the laws of evidence, and international law. Other areas of law are relevant too, for example commercial law (as it relates to advertising), and general press and media law. It is necessary to understand, though, that the law inevitably lags behind technology. There are not definitive legal answers to many of the problems posed: it is a question of having to await new legislation, new or renegotiated international treaties, and new judicial interpretation of existing law.

Copyright Considerations

The UK copyright laws, now enshrined mainly in the *Copyright Designs and Patents Act 1988*, provide a fine example of law lagging behind technology. The Act recognised, for the first time, photography as an original and creative art form. A photograph is now held to be a work of art (irrespective of artistic merit), and the photographer is the first owner of the copyright in any photograph he creates. Nominally, therefore, the Act provides legal protection for photographers equal to that of other creative artists. But despite being a very new piece of legislation, it really offers only theoretical rather than practical answers to some of the problems posed by advancing technology. By way of example, did the Act's draughtsmen - or the politicians who debated, amended and enacted it - take any account of the ease with which a colour photograph can be copied (to a very acceptable quality for some purposes) on the new colour laser photocopiers? Certainly any such copying, if done without the authority (or 'licence' as it is known) of the copyright owner, is unlawful, but the practical policing of the Act in this regard is almost impossible, and enforcement cumbersome and expensive, to a degree probably out of all proportion to the damage suffered.

Likewise, it is also a breach of copyright to scan any protected work into a computer without authority ('licence'): but the same practical problems of policing apply. The photographer will almost certainly be wholly unaware of any initial breach of his rights by scanning; he is unlikely to become aware of small scale commercial exploitation of his image; and he may possibly remain unaware even of larger scale commercial exploitation, particularly if this takes place overseas. In the UK, breach of copyright in the course of trade or business is not only a civil matter, for which the injured party may sue for damages, injunctions and other civil remedies, but is also a **criminal** offence, carrying a maximum penalty of an unlimited fine, two years' imprisonment, or both. The criminal aspects of the copyright law have been used in cases of large scale piracy of video films and computer programs, but it is hard to imagine the police giving a high priority to many breach of copyright cases relating to photography. Private prosecution is an option, but the same cost and bureaucratic considerations apply.

The ownership of copyright in an artistic work is a legal and enforceable property right just like any other property right. It is entirely distinct from the ownership of the physical material. Copyright continues in existence for 50 years after the death of its creator - even if the copyright was assigned by the creator during his lifetime - and, if there was no lifetime assignment, it is dealt with on death in accordance with the normal laws of succession.

If a client commissions a photograph, or buys the use of a photograph from a picture library, then that client has the right to use and reproduce that image for the specific purposes, and to the specific extent, agreed. The client will have bought a 'licence' (which, legally, need not be in writing). In the absence of any specific agreement as to the use of a commissioned photograph, then there will be an implied licence to use that image for the purposes for which it was commissioned. Any further or different use will need a further licence. But the ease, speed and 100% fidelity of digital image scanning, storage on computer hard disks and Photo-CD, copying to floppy disk and removable hard drives, and transmission, either physical or digital, combined with the relative inexpense of all of the associated hardware and software, have left photographers vulnerable to those commercial users of images who might be ignorant of the law or positively unscrupulous.

Manipulation and Moral Rights
If we accept the definition of photography given earlier, and that therefore electronic photography has been in existence for over half a century, then electronic manipulation of images is nothing new. Television drama, for example, has used post-production process techniques, with increasingly plausible results, for many years. Foliage can be removed from trees and snow added to transform a summer scene to winter; modern skylines can be removed and an 'old' skyline substituted; rivers can be made to burst their banks to create flood scenes, and individual pylons, telegraph wires and stray aeroplanes can be eliminated. The finished product does not represent truth, but, as it is all in the name of art, nobody questions it as being unethical. Indeed the 'perpetrators' are often the recipients of various industry and professional awards, and rightly so. But there is a scale of ethical acceptability of such manipulation. Such manipulation would, for example, be wholly unethical, and probably criminal, in the case of photographic or film evidence presented in a court of law. Between the two, there are the areas of varying shades of grey, from the light grey of advertising, where an element of 'puff' is expected and accepted, to the much darker grey of news reporting, where manipulation of the truth, although not unknown, is not acceptable, even if not usually criminal.

Recent developments in digital technology have enabled the seamless manipulation of still images. The same ethical considerations apply as apply to manipulation of the moving image: it is still acceptable in art (surely Pablo Picasso and Salvador Dali manipulated the truth in art!); it is acceptable to a degree in advertising photography; it is not acceptable in news reporting; and it can amount to perjury and other crimes in forensic and evidential photography.

There is another aspect to the manipulation of photographic images which needs consideration. Under the terms of the *Copyright, Designs and Patents Act*, the creator of an artistic work (in the case of a photograph, the photographer) has what is termed the 'moral right' not to have the whole or any part of his work subjected to 'derogatory' treatment. Derogatory treatment amounts to any distortion or mutilation of the work, or any treatment which is prejudicial to the honour or reputation of the creator. The photographer has the power and backing of the law to protect those rights. One of the other moral rights is the right to be identified (with certain limited exceptions) as the creator of the work whenever and wherever it is published.

Libel by Photography

If we accept the old cliché that the 'camera never lies', then, by definition, it is impossible to commit a libel by photography alone (given that one of the essential elements of a libel is that it is untrue). In reality, the camera has always been capable of lying; but now, even if the camera does not lie, then it is possible to create the lie by electronic manipulation. This is wholly different from conventional print retouching techniques which can be used, perhaps, to remove skin blemishes and crow's feet from a subject's face: lies none the less, but lies that can be detected on close inspection of the print - and not libellous. The essence of electronic manipulation is that, if expertly done, it can be indiscernible.

It is unusual for a 'conventional' photograph to be libellous by itself, although a conventional photograph can be libellous - and has been held so - in the context in which it is published or in conjunction with a caption. For example, a photograph of an identifiable innocent man approaching the front door of a house, printed alongside a story about businessmen visiting brothels during their lunch breaks, would almost certainly be libellous. Or if the same photograph was published with a caption which read *'The Bailiff Calls'*, then, if it were untrue, and the house could be identified, then the occupier would probably have been libelled. In the case of a photograph which has been electronically manipulated, it is far easier for the photograph itself, in isolation and without a caption, to be libellous.

There was indeed a recent such case in the United States. A young female model was photographed, in a studio, in total isolation, and looking sultry and seductive. She had merely been told that it was to be an advertising shot, and she was paid accordingly. The published ad showed the young model in close and suggestive proximity to two leering young men. The model sued in the US courts and won substantial damages for libel. The two images, of the young woman model and of the two male models, had been electronically combined.

The International Dimension

The ease of global transmission of digitised images means that no single country can adequately legislate to protect and safeguard the interests of those affected by these new technologies, be they the artistic creators, models, or members of the public. Indeed it is doubtful if even international treaties and agreements can satisfactorily cover many of the misuses and abuses that are likely to occur.

So far as copyright law is concerned, however, most countries in the world are signatories to the Berne and Paris Conventions which, in very simplified summary, impose upon signatory countries the obligation to respect and uphold the copyright laws of all other signatory countries. That means that works protected by the UK Copyright Act are similarly protected throughout the world, and that works created under foreign copyright laws are also protected in the UK. Within the European Community, work has already begun to harmonise the various copyright laws of the 12 member states. This will be done in a piecemeal way, commencing with copyright duration. As it is the intention to harmonise upwards rather than to reduce protection to the lowest common denominator, a copyright duration of 70 years post the death of the creator is likely to emerge.

Conclusions

Legislative developments will never be able to keep abreast of technological developments. Given the slow and cumbersome nature of law-making and the negotiation of international treaties, there will always be, at the very least, a time lag. Almost certainly, there will be a permanent efficacy gap too: the difficulties of drafting complex and comprehensive laws are obvious.

Recent developments in electronic photography have widened considerably the scope for the misuse of images and the abuse of the lawful rights of photographers and others. Sadly, though, the law will be found wanting! And in the absence of enforceable laws in many of these areas, it is incumbent upon the creators and users of photographic images themselves to seek to agree voluntary codes of practice and to recognise the rights of the others. This will require goodwill, strong and representative associations, and honour and integrity all round. Will it actually happen?

APPENDIX 1

SAMPLE TERMS AND CONDITIONS OF BUSINESS
WEDDING AND PORTRAIT PHOTOGRAPHY

These sample terms and conditions of business are given as a guide only. Not all of the following paragraphs will be applicable in all cases; and there will be other factors not covered here that may be of relevance to individual businesses. In as much as they are applicable and appropriate, the following paragraphs may be copied word-for-word, but may not be photocopied.

General

1. The placing of an order by the Client(s) and the acceptance of that order by *[XYZ Photography]* brings into being a contract on *[XYZ Photography's]* terms and conditions as detailed in the following paragraphs.

2. All orders shall be in writing on *[XYZ Photography's]* standard booking form and shall be signed by the Client(s). No terms or conditions relating to any detail of the booking that are not included on the standard booking form shall be binding on *[XYZ Photography]*.

3. In exceptional circumstances, and entirely at its own discretion, *[XYZ Photography]* may accept an order given orally by an existing or former Client who has had notice of these terms and conditions; and these terms and conditions shall apply equally to an order given and accepted orally.

4. In the case of *[XYZ Photography]* accepting an order given orally, the Client(s) shall complete a standard booking form as soon as practicable and, in the absence of completed standard booking form, *[XYZ Photography]* shall accept no liability for any error in executing the order.

5. *[XYZ Photography]* reserves the absolute right to refuse to accept any order whatsoever and for whatever reason, and particularly in cases where *[XYZ Photography]* has reason to believe that acceptance and execution of the order will lead to a breach by *[XYZ Photography]* of the laws of obscenity, libel or copyright, or to the aiding, abetting or condoning of such a breach by any other party.

Cancellation – Wedding Photography

6. In the event of the Client(s) cancelling a booking for wedding photography, *[XYZ Photography]* reserves the right to charge a cancellation fee in accordance with the following scale:

    (i)   20% of the agreed fee if cancelled more than 12 months prior to the wedding date;

    (ii) 35% of the agreed fee if cancelled between six and 12 months prior to the wedding date;

    (iii) 50% of the agreed fee if cancelled less than six months prior to the wedding date;

    (iv) 100% of the agreed fee if cancelled within one month of the wedding date.

Cancellation – Portrait Photography

7. In the event of the Client(s) cancelling a booking for portrait photography, *[XYZ Photography]* reserves the right to charge a cancellation fee of up to twice the agreed sitting fee.

Prices

8. The price list published from time to time by *[XYZ Photography]* shall be inclusive of Value Added Tax or shall prominently and clearly state that the prices are subject to the addition of VAT at the rate for the time being in force.

9. The price payable by the Client(s) for the photography and prints shall be in accordance with *[XYZ Photography's]* price list ruling at the time that the photography is undertaken, not at the time of booking. However, *[XYZ Photography]* shall notify the Client(s) as soon as practicable of any increase in prices between the time of booking and the time of the photography, and the Client(s) shall have the right to cancel the booking without penalty (except that this provision shall not apply to price increases due

solely to an increase in the rate of VAT). Prices for albums, frames and other third party accessories shall be in accordance with prices prevailing at the time of completion of the order.

Methods of Payment

10. In respect of wedding photography, the Client(s) shall pay a deposit of £50 (inclusive of VAT) at the time of booking. The balance of the booking fee shall be due and payable 30 days prior to the date of the wedding. Payment in respect of additional orders for prints, albums and frames placed after the wedding shall be made in full at the time the order is placed.

11. In respect of portrait photography, payment of the sitting fee shall be made in full at the time of booking. Payment in respect of additional orders for prints, albums and frames placed after the portrait session shall be made in full at the time the order is placed.

12. Settlement of accounts shall be by cash, cheque or credit card (Visa, MasterCard). All cheques shall be payable to *[XYZ Photography]*. In the event of a cheque not being honoured on first presentation, for whatever reason, *[XYZ Photography]* reserves the right to charge an administration fee of £15 (plus VAT), and a further £15 (plus VAT) for each subsequent re-presentation of the cheque.

Liability

13. *[XYZ Photography]* will take all reasonable care in the execution of the photography. In the event of a failure outside of the control of *[XYZ Photography]*, the liability of *[XYZ Photography]* shall be limited to a full refund of all money paid in respect of that booking.

14. It shall be the responsibility of the Client(s) to ensure adequate and appropriate insurance cover against any failure of the photography, howsoever caused.

Accuracy of Size and Colour Matching

15. All sizes quoted are nominal and may be subject to a margin of error. *[XYZ Photography]* shall accept no liability for such minor variations in size.

16. The Client(s) accept(s) that fine colour matching is subjective, and that totally accurate colour matching to 100% fidelity is rarely possible. However, *[XYZ Photography]* will endeavour to achieve the closest possible colour match within the limitations of materials and processes used.

Copyright

17. The copyright in all photography created by *[XYZ Photography]* shall be and shall remain the property of *[XYZ Photography]* in accordance with the *Copyright, Designs and Patents Act 1988*. The Client(s) shall have no right to reproduce, or to authorise the reproduction of, by any means whatsoever (including by photocopying or by copying on to film or video tape), any photography created by *[XYZ Photography]*. The Client(s) hereby acknowledge(s) that infringement of *[XYZ Photography's]* copyright is unlawful and may be a criminal offence.

18. The Client(s) hereby agree(s) that any photographs taken by *[XYZ Photography]* may be submitted to any photographic exhibition or competition, or to any newspaper, magazine or other periodical with a view to publication, displayed in a portfolio of work, or otherwise used by *[XYZ Photography]* for promotional purposes.

Ownership of Negatives and Prints

19. All photographic negatives created by *[XYZ Photography]* shall remain the property of *[XYZ Photography]*, and *[XYZ Photography]* undertakes to file and store all such negatives safely and to make them available for future reproduction. Photographic prints will become and remain the property of the Client(s). However, for the avoidance of doubt, the Client(s) specifically acknowledge(s) that ownership of prints does not imply ownership of the copyright in the images on them (which remains the property of *[XYZ Photography]*) or any right to reproduce, or authorise the reproduction of, such images.

Copying of Photography and other Artistic Works

20. In commissioning *[XYZ Photography]* to copy any existing photographic or other artistic work, the Client(s) certify(ies) and warrant(s) that

    (i)   no copyright exists in the material(s); or

    (ii) that he is the owner of the copyright in the material(s) and that any reproduction by *[XYZ Photography]* will not infringe the rights of any existing licensee; or

    (iii) that he has the valid authority of the copyright owner to authorise the reproduction of the material(s) as required by the order.

SAMPLE TERMS AND CONDITIONS OF BUSINESS
INDUSTRIAL AND COMMERCIAL PHOTOGRAPHIC STUDIOS

(The assistance and cooperation of Walter Gardiner Photography, Worthing, and Mr Michael Hemsley FBIPP is gratefully acknowledged.)

These sample terms and conditions of business are given as a guide only. Not all of the following paragraphs will be applicable in all cases; and there will be other factors not covered here that may be of relevance to individual businesses. In as much as they are applicable and appropriate, the following paragraphs may be copied word-for-word, but may not be photocopied.

General

1. The placing of an order by the Client and the acceptance of that order by *[XYZ Studios]* brings into being a contract on *[XYZ Studios']* terms and conditions as detailed in the following paragraphs.

2. With the exception of the specific details of any individual order (for example, as to size, quantity and finish), other terms and conditions proffered by the Client are specifically excluded, unless agreed beforehand in writing by *[XYZ Studios]*.

3. All orders shall be in writing on the Client's official order form or letterhead, and shall be signed by the Client or, in the case of a firm or company, by a responsible person representing the Client.

4. In exceptional circumstances, and entirely at its own discretion, *[XYZ Studios]* may accept an order given orally by an existing or former client

who has had notice of these terms and conditions; and these terms and conditions shall apply equally to an order given and accepted orally.

5. In the case of *[XYZ Studios]* accepting an order given orally, the Client shall confirm such order in writing as soon as practicable and, in the absence of written confirmation, *[XYZ Studios]* shall accept no liability for any error in executing the order.

6. *[XYZ Studios]* reserves the absolute right to refuse to accept any order whatsoever and for whatever reason, and particularly in cases where *[XYZ Studios]* has reason to believe that acceptance and execution of the order will lead to a breach by *[XYZ Studios]* of the laws of obscenity, libel or copyright, or to the aiding, abetting or condoning of such a breach by any other party.

Cancellation

7. In the event of the Client cancelling a commission, *[XYZ Studios]* reserves the right to charge a cancellation fee of 50% of the agreed fee, plus any additional cancellation charges made by Models, Stylists, Set Builders and other third party contractors. Half of any cancellation fee charged by *[XYZ Studios]* shall be credited to the Client in respect of that Client's next commission.

Price, Payments and Accounts

Prices
8. The price payable by the Client for the execution of any order shall be in accordance with *[XYZ Studios']* price list ruling at the time of acceptance of the order. *[XYZ Studios]* reserves the right to alter its price list at any time and without notice.

9. The price list published from time to time by *[XYZ Studios]* is exclusive of Value Added Tax. VAT at the current applicable rate will be added to all charges.

10. *[XYZ Studios]* reserves the right to make additional charges when completion of an order necessitates overtime, weekend or bank holiday working.

11. All accounts shall be settled in full by the Client within 30 days of the date of the invoice.

12. Any account that remains outstanding 30 days after the due date for payment may be referred to a Credit Reference or Collection Agency without further notice to the Client.

13. *[XYZ Studios]* reserves the right to add interest to any account overdue beyond the permitted 30 days at the rate of 2.5% per month.

Cash Accounts

14. *[XYZ Studios]* reserves the right to accept certain commissions strictly on a cash payment basis. In such cases, payment shall be due immediately, as agreed between *[XYZ Studios]* and the Client, and shall be either on a Cash With Order or a Cash On Delivery basis

Methods of Payment

15. Settlement of account invoices shall be by cash or cheque. Cash accounts are payable by cash, cheque or credit card (Visa, MasterCard). All cheques shall be payable to *[XYZ Studios]*. In the event of a cheque not being honoured on first presentation, for whatever reason, *[XYZ Studios]* reserves the right to charge an administration fee of £15 (plus VAT), and a further £15 (plus VAT) for each subsequent re-presentation of the cheque.

Liability

16. *[XYZ Studios]* will take all reasonable care in the handling of all property belonging to, or lawfully in the possession of, the Client. The liability of *[XYZ Studios]* for loss of or damage to such property, however caused, shall be limited to a maximum of £50 (exclusive of VAT) per commission. *[XYZ Studios]* shall not be liable for any consequential losses, special damages, or other indirect losses, howsoever arising.

17. It shall be the responsibility of the Client to ensure adequate and appropriate insurance cover for any property deposited with *[XYZ Studios]* for the purposes of the commission or in transit to or from *[XYZ Studios]*.

18. Unless otherwise specifically agreed by *[XYZ Studios]* in writing, any date or time specified for the completion of a commission, whether by the Client or by *[XYZ Studios]*, shall be an estimate only, and *[XYZ Studios]* shall not be liable for any loss to the Client or to any third party resulting from any reasonable delay in completing the commission.

Accuracy of Size and Colour Matching

19. All sizes quoted are nominal and may be subject to a margin of error. *[XYZ*

Studios] shall accept no liability for such minor variations in size.

20. The Client accepts that fine colour matching is subjective, and that totally accurate colour matching to 100% fidelity is rarely possible. However, *[XYZ Studios]* will endeavour to achieve the closest possible colour match within the limitations of materials and processes used.

Indemnity

21. The Client shall indemnify *[XYZ Studios]* against all third party actions, costs, damages, losses and other claims of whatever nature arising out of the execution of the commission in accordance with the Client's instructions.

Copyright

Original Photography

22. The copyright in all original photography created by *[XYZ Studios]* shall be and shall remain the property of *[XYZ Studios]* in accordance with the *Copyright, Designs and Patents Act 1988.*

The Client's Licence

23. Upon receipt of full payment for a commission in accordance with these terms and conditions, *[XYZ Studios]* shall grant to the Client, inclusive within the price agreed for the commission, a licence to reproduce the photography in any non-photographic form for the purposes and to the extents agreed in writing between *[XYZ Studios]* and the Client. (The 'extents' refers to the time, geographical, and quantity extent agreed.) Any further photographic reproduction shall be carried out only by *[XYZ Studios]*.

24. Any extension to the terms of the licence beyond the purposes and extents agreed shall be subject to negotiation and further agreement between the Client and *[XYZ Studios]*.

25. A licence to reproduce the photography (for the purposes and to the geographical and quantity extents agreed) during the period between completion of the commission and full payment in accordance with these terms and conditions is hereby granted by *[XYZ Studios]* and may be revoked by *[XYZ Studios]* at any time. Specifically, such a licence shall cease automatically in the event of the Client becoming insolvent, ceasing to trade for any other reason, or (if a limited company) going into receivership.

Credits and By-Lines

26. The Client undertakes to ensure that the name of the photographer is published alongside the photography whenever and wherever the photography is reproduced. This legal right of the photographer under the *Copyright, Designs and Patents Act 1988* is hereby asserted.

Ownership of Materials

27. All materials on which original photographic images are created by *[XYZ Studios]* shall remain the property of *[XYZ Studios]*, and *[XYZ Studios]* undertakes to file and store all such original materials safely and to make them available for future reproduction. Where *[XYZ Studios]* gives possession of original transparencies to the Client, such original transparencies shall nevertheless remain the property of *[XYZ Studios]*, and shall be given to the Client on free loan for the duration of the copyright licence. Photographic prints (whether from negatives or transparencies) will become and remain the property of the Client. However, the Client specifically acknowledges that ownership of any physical materials such as prints and transparencies does not imply ownership of the copyright in the images on them (which remains the property of *[XYZ Studios]*) or any right to reproduce or authorise the reproduction of any such images by any photographic means.

Copying of Photography and other Artistic Works

28. In commissioning *[XYZ Studios]* to copy any existing photographic or other artistic work, the Client certifies and warrants that

(i) no copyright exists in the material(s); or

(ii) that he is the owner of the copyright in the material(s) and that any reproduction by *[XYZ Studios]* will not infringe the rights of any existing licensee; or

(iii) that he has the valid authority of the copyright owner (or of an existing licensee of the copyright owner) to authorise the reproduction of the material(s) as required by the order.

29. The Client acknowledges that breach of copyright in the course of trade or business is both a civil wrong and a criminal offence under the terms of the *Copyright, Designs and Patents Act 1988*.

Delivery

30. Delivery of completed orders will be by *[XYZ Studios']* own delivery drivers, or by taxi-cab, courier motorcycle, British Rail Red Star or any other courier or delivery service at the discretion of *[XYZ Studios]*. Where applicable, *[XYZ Studios]* will charge for postage, packing and delivery as appropriate.

31. *[XYZ Studios]* shall not be liable for any damage to, discrepancies in or shortages of delivered materials unless notified by the client within 48 hours of delivery. If *[XYZ Studios]* is so notified within 48 hours, all materials delivered, together with all associated paperwork, shall be returned to *[XYZ Studios]* as soon as practicable.

APPENDIX 3

SAMPLE TERMS AND CONDITIONS OF BUSINESS
PROFESSIONAL PHOTOGRAPHIC LABORATORIES

(The assistance and cooperation of Harrow Photolabs and Mr John Rose HonFBIPP is gratefully acknowledged)

These sample terms and conditions of business are given as a guide only. Not all of the following paragraphs will be applicable in all cases; and there will be other factors not covered here that may be of relevance to individual businesses. In as much as they are applicable and appropriate, the following paragraphs may be copied word-for-word, but may not be photocopied.

General

1. The placing of an order by a client and the acceptance of that order by *[XYZ Photolabs]* brings into being a contract on *[XYZ Photolabs']* terms and conditions as detailed in the following paragraphs.

2. With the exception of the specific details of any individual order (for example, as to size, quantity and finish), other terms and conditions proffered by the Client are specifically excluded, unless agreed beforehand in writing by *[XYZ Photolabs]*.

3. All orders shall be in writing on the Client's official order form or letterhead, and shall be signed by the Client or, in the case of a firm or company, by a responsible person representing the Client.

4. In exceptional circumstances, and entirely at its own discretion, *[XYZ Photolabs]* may accept an order given orally by an existing or former client

who has had notice of these terms and conditions; and these terms and conditions shall apply equally to an order given and accepted orally.

5. In the case of *[XYZ Photolabs]* accepting an order given orally, the Client shall confirm such order in writing as soon as practicable and, in the absence of written confirmation, *[XYZ Photolabs]* shall accept no liability for any error in executing the order.

6. *[XYZ Photolabs]* reserves the absolute right to refuse to accept any order whatsoever and for whatever reason, and particularly in cases where *[XYZ Photolabs]* has reason to believe that acceptance and execution of the order will lead to a breach by *[XYZ Photolabs]* of the laws of obscenity, libel or copyright, or to the aiding, abetting or condoning of such a breach by any other party.

Price, Payments and Accounts

Prices
7. The price payable by the Client for the execution of any order shall be in accordance with *[XYZ Photolabs']* price list ruling at the time of acceptance of the order. *[XYZ Photolabs]* reserves the right to alter its price list at any time and without notice.

8. The price list published from time to time by *[XYZ Photolabs]* is exclusive of Value Added Tax. VAT at the current applicable rate will be added to all charges.

9. *[XYZ Photolabs]* reserves the right to make additional charges when completion of an order is required within 24 hours or necessitates overtime working.

Credit Accounts
10. If the Client shall spend over £500 per month (exclusive of VAT), and at the absolute discretion of *[XYZ Photolabs]*, *[XYZ Photolabs]* will open a client credit account upon receipt of two satisfactory trade references. The continuance of account facilities will be kept under review in the light of the continued value of the orders per month and the manner in which the account is conducted. Withdrawal of account facilities from the Client shall be at the absolute discretion of *[XYZ Photolabs]*.

11. All accounts shall be settled in full by the Client within 30 days of the date of the invoice.

12. Any account with an outstanding balance of more than £250 (inclusive of VAT) and which is overdue by more than 60 days may be referred to a Credit Reference or Collection Agency without further notice to the Client.

13. *[XYZ Photolabs]* reserves the right to add interest to any account overdue beyond the permitted 30 days at the rate of 2.5% per month.

Cash Accounts
14. Where no credit account facility exists, payment terms shall be Cash With Order or Cash On Delivery.

Methods of Payment - Credit Accounts and Cash Accounts
15. Settlement of credit account invoices shall be by cash or cheque. Cash accounts are payable by cash, cheque or credit card (Visa, MasterCard). All cheques shall be payable to *[XYZ Photolabs]*. In the event of a cheque not being honoured on first presentation, for whatever reason, *[XYZ Photolabs]* reserves the right to charge an administration fee of £15 (plus VAT), and a further £15 (plus VAT) for each subsequent re-presentation of the cheque.

Liability

16. *[XYZ Photolabs]* will take all reasonable care in the handling and processing of all materials belonging to the Client.

17. The liability of *[XYZ Photolabs]* for loss of or damage to the Client's materials, however caused, shall be limited to a maximum of £50 (exclusive of VAT) per order. *[XYZ Photolabs]* shall not be liable for any consequential losses, special damages or other indirect losses, howsoever arising.

18. It shall be the responsibility of the Client to ensure adequate and appropriate insurance cover in the event of the value of materials in any one order exceeding £50. It shall also be the responsibility of the Client to insure any goods or original materials deposited with *[XYZ Photolabs]* for the purposes of the order or in transit to or from *[XYZ Photolabs]*.

19. Unless otherwise specifically agreed by *[XYZ Photolabs]* in writing, any date or time specified for the completion of an order, whether by the Client or by *[XYZ Photolabs]*, shall be an estimate only, and *[XYZ Photolabs]* shall not be liable for any loss to the client or to any third party resulting from any reasonable delay in completing the order.

Accuracy of Size and Colour Matching

20. All sizes quoted are nominal and may be subject to a margin of error. *[XYZ Photolabs]* shall accept no liability for such minor variations in size.

21. The Client accepts that fine colour matching is subjective, and that totally accurate colour matching to 100% fidelity is rarely possible. However, *[XYZ Photolabs]* will endeavour to achieve the closest possible colour match within the limitations of materials and processes used. Where accurate colour matching is essential, the client shall provide sample materials for use by *[XYZ Photolabs]* as colour matching guides.

Indemnity

22. The Client shall indemnify *[XYZ Photolabs]* against all third party actions, costs, damages, losses and other claims of whatever nature arising out of the execution of the order in accordance with the Client's instructions.

Copyright

23. It shall be the responsibility of the Client to ensure that all materials presented for processing, printing, copying, duplicating or any other process of reproduction are free from any third party claims for breach of copyright or licence.

24. By placing an order with *[XYZ Photolabs]*, the Client certifies and warrants that

    (i)   no copyright exists in the material(s); or

    (ii) that he is the owner of the copyright in the material(s) and that any reproduction by *[XYZ Photolabs]* will not infringe the rights of any existing licensee; or

    (iii) that he has the valid authority of the copyright owner (or of an existing licensee of the copyright owner) to authorise the reproduction of the material(s) as required by the order.

25. The attention of the Client is drawn specifically to Paragraph 23 *(above)* in respect of indemnity.

26. The Client acknowledges that breach of copyright in the course of trade or business is both a civil wrong and a criminal offence under the terms of the *Copyright, Designs and Patents Act 1988*.

Original Photography Created by [XYZ Photolabs]

27. Where the terms of the order require *[XYZ Photolabs]* to create original photography, the copyright in all such photography shall be the property of *[XYZ Photolabs]* in accordance with the *Copyright, Designs and Patents Act 1988*. *[XYZ Photolabs]* shall grant to the Client, at no additional charge, a licence to reproduce the photography in any non-photographic form, in any quantity, and in any part of the world, for a period of three years from the date of the invoice. Any photographic reproduction shall be carried out only by *[XYZ Photolabs]*. Any extension to the licence beyond the three year period shall be subject to negotiation and further agreement between the Client and *[XYZ Photolabs]*.

28. All materials on which original photographic images are created by *[XYZ Photolabs]* shall remain the property of *[XYZ Photolabs]*, and *[XYZ Photolabs]* undertakes to file and store all such original materials safely and to make them available for future reproduction. Where *[XYZ Photolabs]* gives possession of original transparencies to the Client, such original transparencies shall nevertheless remain the property of *[XYZ Photolabs]*, and shall be given to the Client on free loan for the duration of the copyright licence. Photographic prints (whether from negatives or transparencies) will become and remain the property of the Client. However, the Client specifically acknowledges that ownership of any physical materials such as prints and transparencies does not imply ownership of the copyright in the images on them (which remains the property of *[XYZ Photolabs]* in accordance with Paragraph 27 above) or any right to reproduce or authorise the reproduction of any such images by any photographic means.

Delivery

29. Delivery of completed orders will be by *[XYZ Photolabs']* own delivery drivers, or by taxi-cab, courier motorcycle, British Rail Red Star or any other courier or delivery service at the discretion of *[XYZ Photolabs]*. Where applicable, *[XYZ Photolabs]* will charge for postage, packing and delivery as appropriate.

30. *[XYZ Photolabs]* shall not be liable for any damage to, discrepancies in or shortages of delivered materials unless notified by the client within 48 hours of delivery. If *[XYZ Photolabs]* is so notified within 48 hours, all materials delivered, together with all associated paperwork, shall be returned to *[XYZ Photolabs]* as soon as practicable.

Lien and Retention of Title

31. *[XYZ Photolabs]* shall have a general lien on all of the Client's materials in its possession and shall reserve the right to retain any such materials until all moneys due and payable have been received.

32. In the event of non-payment in accordance with these terms and conditions for any original photography created by *[XYZ Photolabs]*, the licence to reproduce the image(s) shall be thereby immediately revoked without any further notice from *[XYZ Photolabs]*, thereby rendering any reproduction of the image(s) by the Client an infringement of copyright, for which *[XYZ Photolabs]* reserves the right to take such legal action as may be appropriate.

APPENDIX 4

SAMPLE STAFF DISCIPLINARY POLICY AND PROCEDURES

Introductory Note

The following sample Policy and Procedures might seem to some to be excessive and bureaucratic, particularly within an industry in which most employment units consist of very small firms or companies. That may be so; and the sample can be adapted to the particular needs and circumstances of smaller employers. None the less, the provision of a Policy and associated Procedures is a statutory requirement of the *Employment Protection (Consolidation) Act 1978.* But more importantly than that, the existence of such a Policy and Procedures can actually be very beneficial, both to the employer and to employees. For the employee, it removes the fear or threat of arbitrary or unfair treatment, whether from his employer or from fellow employees. For the employer, should the need actually arise to dismiss an employee, the Policy and Procedures provide a fair and just framework that, if properly applied, will stand up to close examination at an Industrial Tribunal.

These sample paragraphs are given as a guide only. Not all of them will be applicable in all cases; and there will be other factors not covered here that may be of relevance to individual businesses. In as much as they are applicable and appropriate, the following paragraphs may be copied word-for-word, but may not be photocopied.

POLICY AND PROCEDURES

General

1. It is the wish and expectation of the management of *[the business]* that all employees will at all times conduct themselves and the affairs of *[the busi-*

ness] in a proper, responsible and business-like manner and with integrity and propriety.

2.   In instances in which the conduct of an employee falls below the required and expected standard, it is the right of the management to bring that short-fall to the attention of the employee and to impose an appropriate sanction.

3.   Such sanction may take one of a number of forms:

a.   Suspension without pay;
b.   An oral warning;
c.   A written warning;
d.   A final warning;
e.   Dismissal with notice; or
f.   Instant dismissal without notice.

4.   In any case in which the application of a sanction is contemplated by the management, a fair and proper procedure is to be applied, and the staff member concerned shall have, and be notified of, the right to appeal against the imposition of any such sanction.

Sanctions

Suspension Without Pay
5.   Suspension without pay will normally only be applied whilst further investi-gations are carried out into a serious alleged offence which might result in dismissal. Subsequent reinstatement of pay if the original allegation cannot be substantiated will be a matter entirely at the discretion of the manage-ment in the light of the particular facts and circumstances.

6.   Suspension without pay may also be applied in cases of drunkenness or other unfitness for work. However, it must be fully understood that drunken-ness at work (particularly in cases in which the safety of any person is jeopardised) will normally result in instant dismissal. This lesser sanction will only be applied in cases that are considered to be isolated, out of char-acter and relatively minor; and in such cases, an oral, written or final warning may also be issued in conjunction with the suspension.

Oral Warning
7.   An oral warning may be issued in cases of relatively minor breaches of discipline, (for example, persistent lateness, minor rudeness, or unauthorised absenteeism). An oral warning may also be appropriate in cases in which an

employee's standard of work is less than the management has a right to expect.

8. It should be borne in mind that examples given above of behaviour likely to lead to the issue of an oral warning are not exhaustive; they are only examples. The management fully expects all staff to have a reasonable idea themselves as to whether or not any particular behaviour warrants disciplinary measures.

9. An oral warning, despite its name, will be recorded in writing. If no further warnings are issued within a reasonable time thereafter, the existence of previous oral warnings will be disregarded.

Written Warning

10. A written warning will be issued in cases of more serious breaches of discipline, or if a further warning becomes necessary relatively soon after the previous issue of an oral warning for the same or similar behaviour.

11. A written warning may also be issued in cases of technical or professional incompetence which in turn threatens the financial, technical or professional standing of *[the business]* (even if such a threat does not result in actual damage to *[the business]*).

12. A written warning will be recorded in writing and will remain current for considerably longer than an oral warning. (For example, depending on the nature and extent of the disciplinary breach, an oral warning may remain current for, say, six months, whereas a written warning may remain current for over a year.) It should be noted that these time scales are given as examples: they may be shortened or lengthened dependent upon the particular circumstances and severity of the case and the previous and subsequent employment history of the employee concerned.

Final Warning

13. A final warning may be issued in cases in which the previous issue of a written warning has not had the desired effect of improving the standard of behaviour or workmanship of the employee.

14. A final warning may, if the circumstances warrant it, be issued as a first warning. However, this will only be contemplated in cases in which the disciplinary breach or technical incompetence is sufficiently serious, but falls short of the gross behaviour that would warrant dismissal.

15. Technical or professional incompetence that results in actual damage to the financial, technical or professional standing or integrity of *[the business]* would be likely to attract a final warning.

16. A final warning may remain 'current' for longer than 12 months, dependent upon the nature and seriousness of the offence, but in any case will lapse totally after a period of two years provided that no such similar behaviour or lapse of professional or technical incompetence has occurred during that time.

Dismissal With Notice
17. An employee may be dismissed with notice in cases in which a previous final warning has been issued in relation to the same or similar behaviour, provided that such recurrence is not sufficiently gross as to warrant instant dismissal without notice.

18. In cases of dismissal with notice, the employee concerned may not be required to work during the notice period. However, payment for the notice period will be in full in accordance with the employee's contract of employment (subject to any statutory deductions).

19. In cases of dismissal with notice such as envisaged in paragraph 18 above, the effective date of dismissal shall be the date on which the notice period would have expired had the noticed period been fully served.

Instant Dismissal Without Notice
20. The management of *[the business]* reserves the right to dismiss any employee instantly and without notice in any case of gross misbehaviour, gross technical or professional incompetence, or consequent upon any other act or omission so gross as to represent a fundamental breach of the contract of employment on the part of the employee. In such circumstances, there will be no entitlement to payment in lieu of notice, and any payment actually made to the employee shall be entirely at the discretion of the management and without implying any liability on *[the business]*.

21. Examples of the type of instances that might lead to an employee being instantly dismissed without notice are:

    a.   falsification of company records or accounts;
    b.   being under the influence of alcohol or drugs whilst on company business to such a degree as either to pose a threat to the safety of any person

(including the employee him/herself) or to cause severe embarrassment to *[the business]*;

c.   conviction of any criminal offence which, in the opinion of the management, makes the continued employment of that person undesirable in the interests of *[the business]*;

d.   gross acts of sexual or racial harassment, or similar offensive behaviour, or the use of offensive or insulting behaviour (including the use or threat of violence), towards a colleague, or a client, or any other person encountered in the course of employment;

e.   tampering with any item of safety equipment so as to pose a danger to any person, or reckless as to whether any such danger might be posed;

f.   failure to adhere to and abide by any law, rule or regulation in relation to the health or safety of any person such as to endanger any person or to show recklessness as to whether any person is endangered;

g.   failure to cooperate with the management in the legitimate implementation of any health and safety laws, rules or regulations or of this Disciplinary Policy;

h.   theft or other misappropriation of any money or other property belonging to *[the business]*, a fellow employee, a client, or any other person or body with whom the employee has dealings in the course of employment;

i.   any professional or technical act or omission that causes serious damage to the financial position of *[the business]* or that causes serious damage to the credibility or standing of *[the business]* in the eyes of clients, potential clients, the wider professional photography industry or the general public.

22. It should be noted that the above list is not exhaustive and merely provides examples of the kinds of acts or omissions that might lead to an employee being dismissed instantly from *[the business's]* employment.

Procedures

23. The right to apply any of the disciplinary sanctions shall be vested in *[the proprietor/ a director/the manager/named persons (insert as appropriate)]*.

24. An employee is always to be notified of any alleged occurrence in respect of which a disciplinary sanction is contemplated.

25. The employee shall be given an opportunity to present his/her side of the case and to speak in his/her own defence. When exercising these opportunities, the employee shall be entitled to be accompanied by a colleague and to

present such evidence and to call such witnesses as are reasonable and relevant.

26. An employee to whom a disciplinary sanction is applied shall be advised at the time of the right to appeal against such sanction.

27. Confirmation of any disciplinary sanction applied to an employee shall be given to that employee in writing, and the employee shall acknowledge such confirmation, also in writing. This Rule applies even if the sanction applied is an oral warning.

28. Every employee is to cooperate fully with the implementation of these Disciplinary Procedures. Failure to do so will itself constitute a disciplinary offence and may ultimately, therefore, lead to dismissal.

Rights of Appeal

29. Any employee against whom any of the above disciplinary sanctions has been applied shall have the right to appeal against such sanction.

30. The appeal shall be heard by *[the board of directors/at least two directors/the partners/named persons (insert as appropriate)]*.

31. All of the same procedures shall apply to the hearing of an appeal as apply to the original examination of the case, and the decision of those hearing the appeal shall be final (subject only to any subsequent decision of a court of law or an Industrial Tribunal).

APPENDIX 5

USEFUL ADDRESSES

Agfa-Gevaert Ltd
27 Great West Road
Brentford TW8 9AX
(Telephone 081 560 2131)

Amateur Photographer
King's Reach Tower
Stamford Street
London SE1 9LS

Association of Photographers
9-10 Domingo Street
London EC1Y 0TA
(Telephone 071 608 1441)

British Association of Journalists
97 Fleet Street
London EC4Y 1DH
(Telephone 071 353 3003)

British Association of Picture Libraries and Agencies
13 Woodberry Crescent
London N10 1PJ
(Telephone 081 444 7913)

British Institute of Professional Photography
Fox Talbot House
2 Amwell End, Ware
Hertfordshire SG12 9HN
(Telephone 0920 464011)

British Journal of Photography
186-187 Temple Chambers
Temple Avenue
London EC4Y 0DB

Canon (UK) Ltd (Photo Division)
Brent Trading Centre
North Circular Road
Neasden
London NW10 0JF
(Telephone 081 459 1266)

Champion Photo Chemistry Ltd
Hubert Road
Brentwood
Essex CM14 4QQ
(Telephone 0277 263646)

Companies House
Crown Way
Maindy
Cardiff CF4 3UZ
(Telephone 0222 380529)

Electronic Photo-Imaging Centre
(Training and Consultancy in
Electronic Imaging)
1 Brentford Business Centre
Commerce Road
Brentford TW8 8LG
(Telephone 081 568 7700)

English Nature
Northminster House
Northminster Road
Peterborough
Cambridgeshire PE1 1UA
(Telephone 0733 340345)

Fuji Photo Film (UK) Ltd
Fuji Film House
125 Finchley Road
London NW3 6JH
(Telephone 071 586 5900)

Guild of Wedding Photographers
13 Market Street
Altrincham
Cheshire WA14 1QS
(Telephone 061 926 9367)

Hasselblad (UK) Ltd
York House
Empire Way
Wembley
Middlesex HA9 0QQ
(Telephone 081 903 3435)

Health and Safety Executive
Baynards House
1 Chepstow Place
Westbourne Grove
London W2 4TF
(Telephone 071 221 0870)

Health and Safety Executive
Broad Lane
Sheffield S3 7HQ

Ilford Ltd
14/22 Tottenham Street
London W1P 0AH
(Telephone 071 636 7890)

Institute of Journalists
2 Dock Offices
Surrey Quays
London SE16 2XL
(Telephone 071 252 1187)

Johnsons of Hendon Ltd
Hempstall Lane
Newcastle-under-Lyme
Staffordshire ST5 0SW
(Telephone 0782 717100)

Kodak Ltd
PO Box 66, Station Road
Hemel Hempstead
Hertfordshire HP1 1JU
(Telephone 0442 61122)

Lord Chancellor's Department
Trevelyan House
30 Great Peter Street
London SW1P 2BY
(Telephone 071 210 8500)

Master Photographer
12 Alma Grove
Fulford Road
York YO1 4DH

Master Photographers Association
Hallmark House
97 East Street
Epsom
Surrey KT17 1EA
(Telephone 0372 726123)

**National Museum of Film, Photography
and Television**
Princes View
Bradford
West Yorkshire

National Trust
36 Queen Anne's Gate
London SW1H 9AS
(Telephone 071 222 9251)

National Union of Journalists
314 Grays Inn Road
London WC1X 8DP
(Telephone 071 837 8143)

Panorama
Alexander House
Forehill
Ely
Cambridgeshire CB7 4AF
(Telephone 0353 665577)

Pentax (UK) Ltd
Pentax House
South Hill Avenue
South Harrow
Middlesex HA2 0LT

The Photographer
Fox Talbot House
2 Amwell End
Ware
Hertfordshire SG12 9HN
(Telephone 0920 464011)

PhotoPro
Icon Publications Ltd
Maxwell Place
Maxwell Lane
Kelso
Borders TD5 7BB
(Telephone 0573 226032)

PIC (People in Camera)
Lingley House
Commissioners Road
Strood
Rochester
Kent ME2 4EU

Polaroid (UK) Ltd
Ashley Road
St Albans
Hertfordshire AL1 5PR

Practical Photography
Apex House
Oundle Road
Peterborough PE2 9NP

Professional Photographer
Wenden Court
Wendens Ambo
Saffron Walden
Essex CB11 4LB

**Professional Photographic Laboratories
Association**
9 Deane Avenue
Timperley
Altrincham
Chesire WA15 7QD
(Telephone 061 980 1532)

The Royal Photographic Society
The Octagon
8 Milsom Street
Bath BA1 1DN
(Telephone 0225 462841)

Royal Society for the Protection of Birds
The Lodge
Sandy
Bedfordshire SG19 2DL
(Telephone 0767 680551)

**Society of Picture Researchers and
Editors**
PO Box 259
London WC1N 3XX
(Telephone 071 581 1371)